THE AWAKENER

The Time is Now

SANDY STEVENSON

GATEWAY

Gateway
an imprint of
Gill & Macmillan Ltd
Hume Avenue, Park West
Dublin 12
with associated companies throughout the world
www.gillmacmillan.ie

Revised reprint 1998, 1999, 2000, 2001, 2002
© 1997 Sandy Stevenson

1 85860 040 5

Set in 11 on 13 pt Sabon by
Character Graphics (Taunton) Ltd
Printed by ColourBooks Ltd, Dublin

The paper used in this book comes from the wood pulp of managed
forests. For every tree felled, at least one tree is planted,
thereby renewing natural resources.

A catalogue record is available for this book
from the British Library.

Preface

Perhaps occasionally you look at complicated and intellectualised concepts and feel upset that you cannot grasp the deep meanings of these pearls of wisdom. You may even feel that you are missing some vital data that will take you to great levels of enlightenment. This can be the mind at work, dictating a need to intellectualise and analyse.

The purest of truth is very simple and can be expressed in simple terms that all can understand. In order to be a part of the great event happening now on Earth, you do not need to be a physicist or understand any great universal mystery. No specific religion or race holds the magic key. It is not required that you know when Atlantis sank or the significance of Sirius. You don't need to understand leylines or what crop circles are all about.

All that is required is faith and trust in the perfection of Divine order and to love unconditionally – everything, everyone, everywhere. Every moment you move in faith, trust and love, you are changing the face of Earth and the history of the Universe.

When you move deep within the intuitive knowing of Spirit, you will find that true wisdom has little to do with words. True wisdom comes when we reside in a loving space of Spirit and bring the mind to stillness. As we allow ourselves to feel and experience our connection to a higher Divine order, we encompass a higher Truth that enriches our lives beyond measure.

From a place of Spirit, we are lovingly led to an awareness of a greater picture of life. This movement of Spirit often defies rational explanation, but resides in an unseen world of beauty, wonder and pure truth.

One of the wonderful gifts of Spirit is our ability to discern differing energies and levels of truth. A feeling of harmony occurs deep within when we are comfortable with concepts that feel true for us. Equally, we may feel ourselves rejecting things that do not resonate with us. To establish either, we need only to listen to our inner voice. From this space of clarity and without confusion, your life and your service to Earth is greatly enhanced.

It is suggested that you apply your inherent gift of discernment to all you read in this book.

DEDICATION

This book is dedicated to all those throughout the Universe who had the incredible love, courage and absolute determination to implement the Divine plan on Earth.

To the God/Creator/All-That-Is/Universal Source, to all the magnificent Cosmic beings and ascended realms of Light in all the universes, to the angels, guides and elementals of all life for the great gifts of their presence, energy, healing and love. To the millions of incredible, invincible starseeds and lightworkers whose value exceeds mathematical calculation, and to all of humanity for the most incredible sustaining power and perseverance in all of universal history.

It is with humble gratitude I thank the Ascended Masters and Cosmic beings for their assistance in helping me experience the great wonders of Spirit and a multi-dimensional world that enabled me to take up my tasks with courage, faith and trust. I thank them for their love, patience and sense of humour.

I also wish to dedicate this book to my beloved twin flame with whom, whilst still in physical form, I shared but a few short days, but who now shares my life from the realms of Spirit, as I complete my tasks on Earth.

Come, toucher of deep in my soul
Let us leap together, beloved.

Freewheeling through time and space
In joy and laughter hugging the moon,
Shaping falling stars into new patterns

Sliding along the glimmer of galaxies' rays
Dancing and leaping over planets
Looking for doorways of universes
Creating golden rainbows in our wake

My Love, my life, my world
All ways Always

For eternity
And beyond and beyond
Lighter and finer.

We have dreamed long
But we have dreamed well
You and I.

SHANTARN – *Sandy Stevenson*

THANK YOU

To my wonderful Mum – Esmé, an old soul as young as ever, whose eyes still twinkle with mischief and whose commitment and loving dedication of service to the Universe is absolute. To my amazing brother Dennis, a master by example – a lifetime without a negative word. Who else would keep their old Valiant car, to ensure the word 'Valiant' remains in the English language on Earth! My beloved daughter Tania, walking in the Light of God, carrying her beauty, wisdom, perception and love throughout the world. You have taught me so much. I would like to say to all my family – it is truly an honour to know and serve with you and I love you unconditionally.

Thank you Australia, my birth place – and England, my spiritual home – for sharing your exquisite beauty with me.

Thank you to the friends who have touched my heart in their sharing of this and past incarnations.

Brian Hasler (for your awakening) and Jono Rogers (for your invaluable help). Thank you both for your integrity in keeping your pre-incarnational agreements.

All the Haslers and the Rogers, Betty, Merlin, O'Le-an and Elonia (Eddie & Crissie Romano), Carole Oleson, Robin Bee, Mathilde, Sally, Renee, Christine, Maurice, Vicky Dixon, Ann Robson, Gaye, Vicky Kingsley, Connie, Helle & Talal, Stephen Davies for bringing an awareness of nutritional medicine to the UK, (Merry Xmas Forever); Doris, Suki, Tai, Bouncer, Suzette, Vicky, the performers on 21 August 94 at Wembley; Maxie, Ginny, Rich, Peter, Joan, Da Vid, Mandy, John, Trudy, Stefan, Carmen, Marcus, Robyn, David, Susan, Lesley – and to just a few of the very many who have touched my heart as I've seen the great help they give to this beloved planet, Solara, Patricia Cota Robles, Oprah Winfrey, Stuart Wilde, Louise Hay – and to John Christian (UK), Matisha (USA) and Chris James (Australia's magical Singing Master) for their wonderful songs that take you 'home'.

Table of Contents

CHAPTER ONE

Earth Mission

The Earth Mother originally undertook an agreement to allow humans to use her body (the Earth) as a school for learning through **limitation**. This agreement was made with great love and compassion and an understanding of the trials that may ensue. It was also to be a learning for the Earth Being herself.

As humanity progressed through this learning, certain negative forces came to this planet and began tampering with the genetic patterns of the plant and animal forms. Prior to this, all the flora and fauna of Earth were beautiful and there were no such things as thorns on roses, stinging nettles, poisonous berries or noxious weeds. These did not develop naturally for the protection of the plants and bushes, for no protection was needed. Animals were changed from herbivores to carnivores. Man began accepting the suggestion that he could achieve greater performance by allowing alterations of his vibrational field, and so the human genetic blueprint was also altered. This permitted greater control by the negative forces and a negative imbalance came into play on Earth. Thus humanity began its greatest learning through limitation in what became **the densest energy planet in the entire Universe.**

Owing to the imbalance of the Earth's energy over a period of time, it became more and more difficult for its inhabitants to progress at what is viewed as a more normal evolutionary rate of learning. Because of the adoption of negative patterns by many on Earth, the entire density was affected. The human population began to lose sight of the truth of its origins. So both the Earth and humanity became entangled in a never ending karmic wheel of learning.

The Earth Mother requested assistance from the universal forces of Light for both herself and humanity and this was heard by the Highest on High.

The Earth needed cleansing from the surplus of negativity, to permit her evolution to higher realms.

The human population needed to be made aware of its true spiritual nature and connection to the Supreme Creator, as well as needing assistance in releasing its negative patterning causing the dense energy.

A call went out across the Universe for 144,000 committed evolved beings who would be willing to perform a series of incarnations upon the Earth, teaching and focusing Light in order to shift the existing imbalance of negative energy present upon Earth. These beings are referred to as the Starseed and are the ones mentioned in the Bible. As many now realise, although the Bible contains a lot of truth, much of it has suffered a great deal of alteration. This has come about both accidentally through language translations, and deliberately in order to maintain control of the people, such as the deletions of references to reincarnation (they missed a few) at the Council of Nicea.

The 144,000 came – from different galaxies and planes of existence – across universes they came, and they met at the designated place on Orion. The gathering was overseered by a great Cosmic being – Lord Sanat Kumara, the Planetary Logos, following the divine instruction of Christ.

Mission agreements were made and contracts signed. These contracts were in the main scheduled for completion toward the end of the 20th century, and prior to the year 2,000.

The figure of 144,000 involved mathematics and required a specific percentage of starseeds to represent their various soul families on Earth. Under the requirements of universal law, if they became inhabitants of Earth, these starseeds would be permitted to make decisions and act on behalf of their soul families. The Universal Law of Non-Intervention (just like the prime directive in Star Trek!) states that no-one, other than the inhabitants of a planet, is permitted to change or alter the evolutionary state of that planet.

There are **three exceptions** to this rule:

1. If one planet is about to destroy another.
2. If a planet is holding up the evolutionary progress of its galaxy. This would mean that a galaxy was ready to evolve into a higher

dimension, but could not because one of its planets was not yet ready.

3. If a planet was about to destroy itself. This newer addition to the law was brought into being about 6,000 years ago, after viewing the position on Earth. It was based on the experience of the planet Maldek (Lucifer) which blew itself up, affecting the entire galaxy.

As parts of Maldek littered the galaxy, Earth ended up with some of its species, such as spiders. Most of Maldek's species were brown or black in colour. If you are one of those people who are frightened of spiders, just think what it has been like for the spiders, traumatically uprooted from home and thrown into a place of alien vibration, where most people upon seeing you threw up their hands in horror and tried to kill you. However as with all things, a learning has taken place on both sides. The spiders have adapted and survived and now many of Earth's population feel friendly toward them, or at least tolerate them.

There is another allowance made regarding the Law of Non-Interference. Under universal law, we have the power to use The Right To Decree (see Chapter 9). This right can be used by any lightworker who is endeavouring to act as a master in service to God. The intention in using it must be pure. It cannot be used to try and earn points. When a lightworker uses this right, it gives permission to the ascended realms of Light to act.

Without this, they are bound by the non-intervention rule. It is of great importance that this right be understood and used extensively to allow the maximum assistance of Light to the planet.

Although it was anticipated that other beings would come forward in the future to assist with the plan for Earth, many starseeds were asked to take up extra tasks, in addition to the main contractual agreements, to allow for all contingencies. It seemed unlikely at the time that these extra-ordinary tasks would actually be needed.

After the starseeds met on Orion and descended to Earth, many other beings began offering their assistance. These beings are often referred to as lightworkers.

Although the Universe is only energy vibrating at different rates, we use the term 'dimension' to bring clarity and understanding.

Beings from various planets, galaxies and dimensions, ranging in evolution from the fourth to the lower seventh, chose to join the team on Earth. Beings from the higher levels of the seventh dimension (such as the Ascended Masters) are not permitted to actually incarnate into a third dimension, because their high vibrational presence may change the evolution of life forms around them. They may however, manifest in etheric form or send an aspect of themselves. The willingness and dedication of the lightworkers and starseeds brought about the greatest reversal in planetary density ever imaginable. In their thousands they came and as time passed they were joined by many more thousands, each making the same basic agreements of commitment to the continued focus of Light on Earth. Now they number millions and are still coming. Those incarnating more recently simply offer Love and Light and have no other mission tasks. You may find you are drawn to make eye contact with these babies and small children. As many of them have never incarnated here before, this contact from an awakened lightworker can register a feeling of safety and rightness in their new world.

Many plans were drawn up arranging different teams to cover many thousands of tasks encompassing every area of life on Earth. The plan involved a series of many incarnations and needed a massive amount of intricate planning, precision timing and a great responsibility, for both the individuals and all the teams involved to uphold their agreements during many lifetimes, in order to achieve the Divine plan.

The plan included an awakening team, due to be awakened themselves and be in place in designated countries by 1991. One task of this team was to help awaken the rest. There is a section at the end of this book that has been written for this group.

The plan to awaken the Light Force involved the use of every type of communication available, including taped channelling, music, dance, sound, essences, vibrational colour, as well as the more traditional methods of books, lectures and workshops. Although it is not always realised, all these methods are used by Spirit, and much of all the wisdom reaching us in all these forms is channelled. Where ego is visibly present, and the data complicated and difficult to understand, this material is usually being given from the viewpoint of the incarnated soul or a lower level channelling source.

The lightbearers of Earth, here to undertake the Divine Will of God, are referred to by many names. Because these names are triggers of memory, some may feel more comfortable with one name than another. Whatever the name, be it the Archangel Michael's legionnaires or eagles, lightworkers and starseeds, lightbearers, rainbow warriors, the Light Force or angels, in truth they are all one and equal.

The Divine plan for Earth is perfect. Conceived in complete unconditional love, it encompasses every life form on Earth, ensuring that all are cared for according to their highest good. Heaven and Earth are combining and Love is coming to Earth. This state is called Ascension.

This plan allows for the Earth to graduate to a higher dimension in accordance with the Divine Will of God. It was to be given assistance by the universal Light Forces, both incarnate and discarnate. These forces consist of groups known as the White Brotherhood, the Ascended Masters, Cosmic beings, the archangels and angelic realms, the deva and elemental world (the veils have now been lifted between the elemental and the human worlds), the people of the inner Earth (many of whom are 5th and 6th dimensional beings), the Space Brotherhood, the Galactic Confederation's fleet of spaceships, planetary systems such as Sirius, the Light Forces of the Pleiades constellation (a system still in duality), Essasani, and the many planets of Light wishing to help with the birth of Earth into her new dimension of Light. There are also space fleets from systems outside the galaxy who wish to contribute, but as their ships are too large to enter our galactic doorway, they help by beaming Light toward Earth. All those not classed as inhabitants of the Earth require permission from the incarnated Light Force in order to assist.

The blueprint of the Divine plan never changes, nor do the original agreements made in the contract. Due to 'free will and choice' which is available to all, some aspects within the overall plan do change. If it has become more desirable to change direction or some detail in a plan, then a meeting is called and the team members concerned discuss and re-plan if necessary. This could occur when a task has been completed more quickly than anticipated. Occasionally it may be that a center or healing therapy that was previously with the Light, has been taken over by someone working with negative energies. Such a place would aim to attract lightworkers, so they often offer special or glamorous services that are not commonly available. This could range from workshops on learning how to channel, pampered retreats or claiming that their place has some special energy to offer. Naturally, genuine Light centres also offer such things, so use intuition as your guidance.

These meetings occur on a higher dimension and take place during the sleep state, when all souls on Earth connect to the spiritual realms. You might feel you were on your correct path, but if this area has now cleared and you are no longer needed there, you will suddenly find yourself with a blank screen, unsure of your next move. This blank screen allows you to regroup and gives you time to let go of any fixed patterns you may have formed. As this letting go takes place, another path begins to show itself. It may be that your own original agreements involve a series of different tasks, often in unrelated areas. If you are able to easily change and follow your excitement in faith and trust, then the new path would be instantly manifest. A feeling of excitement will confirm the right move for you to make in each moment. It is very important however, to be specific about this by observing exactly which aspect of something excites you. You may hear of a workshop being given on colour healing in a specific place and feel excited. Just check to see which aspect it is exactly that you feel excited about. Is it the colour, the healing, the location or something else that attracted your attention and caused the excitement?

Because all the starseeds and the majority of lightworkers have previously evolved to the fifth dimension or above, they have already formed a light body, which is the vehicle for the fifth, much as the solid body is for the third dimension.

Although all the starseed and the majority of lightworkers have ascended before to a fifth dimension (some to the 6th) at some point prior to coming on this Earth mission, this is the first opportunity to ascend with the physical form (See Chapter 4) and from this level of density. Each evolvement that takes one to a new higher dimension could be called a level of ascension, with the 5th dimension being thought of as the first level. The Ascended Masters, for example, have ascended to the higher sections of the 7th dimension.

The smaller percentage of lightworkers who came in from the fourth dimension are currently in the process of forming their light body, along with those of humanity choosing to do so, for their first ascension to the 5th dimension. This will take place naturally as the clearing process takes place and their vibratory rate increases.

It is a great limitation for beings to incarnate into the third density from higher levels of awareness and freedom. Many of the Light Force came from almost unimaginably exquisite places, living in bodies of shimmering light with 360 degree vision and pure knowing. To leave this and take form in the confinement of a solid third dimensional body with all its restrictions, vulnerability and limited perceptions, is quite an act of mastery in itself. To then be immersed even further into the density by adopting the limiting patterns and relevant doctrines of many cultures, is truly an act of service.

This process was set to coincide with the completion of many other major universal cycles and would establish itself over a twenty year period due to end by 2011. This year also marks the end of the Egyptian, Tibetan and Mayan calendars. The coming time is known as the Age of Aquarius, 2,000 years of peace and harmony and the time of 'I Know'. We are just completing the Age of Pisces, the time of 'I Believe'. This was a 2,000 year cycle introduced by Jesus, for humanity to begin to understand compassion and the concept that we are as brother and sister. The period prior to that was the Age of Aries, 'I am'.

We find prophecies about the ending of Earth have been made in many old religions and civilisations. Often symbolic concepts have been translated through a third dimensional understanding and produce fearful forecasts of destruction. In truth, what **is** ending is the pain and suffering and the pattern of learning through limitation. It is an old way of life that is completing on Earth and a new learning is beginning that contains the God qualities of love, harmony, integrity, service and peaceful coexistence. One name this has is the Christ Consciousness, not to imply a limited religious definition, but to embody an awareness that we are spiritual beings and connected to a Divine universal consciousness. These calendars ending in 2011 may well signify the final completion point of the last remnants of third and fourth dimensional ways of life.

So allowing for the free will and choice of Mother Earth to determine the process and route she takes, we could perhaps see this planet birthed into her new dimensions in 2012. This would be the birth of a wondrous, long awaited new age where all on Earth will be aware of their Divine connection and will live their lives in truth as Spirit. This would mean that all cleansing, balancing and transmuting of any lower frequencies would have taken place.

This particular incarnation we are all in is the most important. All the extensive preparation throughout many lifetimes now brings this period to its successful completion. Within the time frame of the last few years of this century, the majority of missions end and the Light Force returns home. The sceptres are now being passed to the holders of the forthcoming age. It was never necessary for the Light Force to remain here until the Earth births fully into her new dimension.

Whilst lightworkers and starseeds have been born at **all times** throughout the past 90 or so years, there have also been key times for mass incarnations.

In the period between 1910 and 1925 a number of starseeds incarnated carrying information to begin awakening the Light Force. This group included wonderful beings such as Sir George Trevelyan, founder of the Wrekin Trust in the UK and pioneer of a great spiritual awakening. These wonderful trail blazers often had a tough time. Not only did they have to handle the controversy that often arises when cutting new ground, the majority didn't have the advantage of being born into starseed or lightworker families, as did all those who followed.

Perhaps you are saying 'I was born after 1925 and I don't think my family are lightworkers'. If you have thought this, perhaps you haven't looked at the higher picture. In spite of what you may think, from a higher perspective you will see that your family is really helping you release or overcome something, and you are helping them. Often it is those who love you the most who are willing to make the greatest sacrifice. These are the ones who will play out the mean father, the unfaithful lover, the spouse beater and even the murderer.

The majority of starseeds and many lightworkers incarnated around the end of World War Two. Many had been involved in the war, completing agreements and balancing out their karma. Most of this particular group, as well as the 1910 group, have been here for the longest period of the mission and had a great amount of clearing to do. As they go through all the releasing, initiations, testing, merging with the I AM and becoming multi-dimensional, it may seem at times to friends and family that there is an unstable person let loose. With all the strange things that happen, it could certainly make one wonder! However, usually hidden away underneath any chaos is the realisation that all is in order and that for some reason (usually completely obscure and impossible to comprehend), you know this is all necessary. You are some of the toughest beings in the entire Universe and it is with great respect and incredulous disbelief that many of other planetary systems view the wonderful endurance achieved here by the Light Force.

Then around the 1965 to 1973 period, a large number of lightworkers incarnated, many very highly evolved. They are masters, as are the majority of the Light Force. Some of them are starchildren and these evolved beings often have an air of innocence or vulnerability about them. Most are not familiar with the patterns of Earth and can have difficulty with the emotions and the games played out on Earth. From the parents' point of view, they can appear to be entangled in emotional dramas and the materialistic side of life. This is mainly because they try to quickly learn the Earth patterns in order to establish an understanding and reality of the life here, so that they are able to identify with those they are meant to assist.

These beings are masters from higher planes of finer vibrations (often other planetary systems). Because they are not used to this density with its harsher vibrations, they often feel they don't belong here and can feel quite lonely. It helps them if their parents are aware of their situation and can give loving guidance that will assist them to relate to this world. These ones generally have specific mission tasks, in addition to that of spreading Love and Light across the planet. In many cases, one of their tasks is to help awaken their starseed parents.

Whereas it is not common to change evolutionary paths, special dispensations have been given to allow many beings to do so at this time. Many angels and gnomes are incarnated now. Angels also incarnate at other times, although it is not common. When a being has completed all the learning on their existing evolutionary path, he or she may request, and be granted, permission to change from the angelic kingdom learning path to the human path or vice versa. Mother Mary was from the angelic realms prior to incarnating as Jesus' mother. She was tested intensely for this role, being required to hold the focus of Light unwaveringly for many, many years, including a long period alone in the wilderness. This was to ensure that she could be depended upon to hold the Light throughout the incarnate lifetime of Jesus.

A further influx of lightworkers came to Earth in the years around 1988 and these ones maintain an awareness of their connection to the Source. If you hand them a crystal, most respond instantly. Many of these are also starchildren, but are here simply to focus love and channel Light. Of this group, those who have incarnated recently cannot be classed as Earth inhabitants and therefore have no additional mission task other than the spreading of love and Light wherever they go. Most are aware that they will not be very long in this density. A few will stay for one brief lifetime to assist those who will do their learning on this fifth dimensional planet, following Earth's ascension.

All the babies born into lightworker families since 1992 are themselves lightworkers, but usually have no other task than the focus of love and Light. They have an even greater conscious awareness of who they truly are than those born between 1965 and 1973. They also know they will not be here for long.

It is worth mentioning that the majority of the lightworkers born since 1965 do not need the same waking up procedures as the longer term missionaries. They have not taken on the great mass of third dimensional conditioning, nor do they need waking up from a long deep sleep. So, whereas the longer term starseeds and lightworkers may find the awakening process and the concept of ascension very exciting, don't be surprised if these younger ones find it all a bit boring or 'over the top'. They can do without the workshops, clearing techniques, books and lectures that provide so much for a large percentage of the Light Force. Some may find themselves arguing with their children about their seeming lack of interest in ascension. You may be disappointed at your child's failure to support the steps you take to reattain your identity. Please realise that the majority have no idea what it feels like to have gone through the entire process. Flare-ups can also occur as they protest at being told they 'should' read this book or 'need' to go to that lecture or at being made to feel guilty about their lack of response to things you may think are 'better than sliced bread'. They can't duplicate your excitement that it is all really happening at last. They also do not understand your deep weariness or the longing to go home. They do also want to go home, but for most of them it is more of a flippant "OK, when I've had enough of this, I'll get out of here". Many of this group want to 'see and do absolutely everything' before they leave, and are rushing to get it all done in time.

They are also masters and you must trust they will find their path in their own way and in their time, just as you did. However it will probably be their way and not the way you chose. That does not prevent you from intuitively guiding them, because they often really need guidance. Because they are spiritually evolved, any tactful mention of an applicable spiritual truth can really assist them quickly to gain the correct perspective they need. Prearranged agreements exist for you to be their parents because of your good grasp of Earth procedures and they knew they would be in safe hands while they 'learned the ropes'. Because it is your role to teach them and you take that agreement seriously, it is easy to slip into the role of always correcting them. Don't forget to also lovingly acknowledge them for all the areas of life in which they are succeeding; they need this from you. If you can understand where they are 'coming from', you will find it easier to love and support them through the difficulties they may be experiencing with this density. They are usually very intuitive and perceptive and, if allowed to follow their own guidance, will move very precisely on their path.

It is not very different from a normal parent/child relationship, except that both of you are masters. You are now awakening and remembering who you are. They have always had a conscious awareness of a deep and profound connection to the Source, even though they may never mention it or even know how to voice it. They have an inherent knowing that they will ascend when they are finished here. They wouldn't perhaps call it ascension as you understand it. It is an unconscious knowing, so they will often not respond to the material being issued about ascension.

The processes that are needed to cause an awakening vary among the Light Force. This depends on the route one has taken to arrive here, where one originated from prior to entry here, and how long one has been here.

Our domestic pets are another part of the Light Force that work closely with us. You will find that many old soul animals have incarnated in this particular lifetime. Often your cat or dog has been with you many times before and has come to give you support in this last time on Earth. You can often see the great wisdom in the eyes of these ones – the eyes truly being the 'windows of the soul' for all life.

Most of the Light Force also have other mission functions which occur in the spiritual realms during your sleep time. If you do not recall what you are doing in the night, there are several valid reasons for this. It is not because you aren't evolved enough or clever enough to remember! You may have decided along with your 'I Am' presence, that it is more beneficial for the greater good of the mission that you do not remember the events of the evening, for the following reasons:

1. Most of the Light Force is going through the process of releasing their weariness. This is accompanied by the desire to leave that comes always in the last stages of a mission. From the higher perspective of your sleep state, you have realised that if you remembered the perceptions of the higher realms, it would be more difficult for you to be willing to remain in this density until your mission is completed.

2. It has also been calculated that it would take most people until around 2pm each day to get grounded again. This would seriously affect your ability to do your task and would effect the mission as a whole. If you are thinking that your angels or guides could help you make that adjustment, you are correct. However, this is the time on Earth when you pick up your mastership.

3. The other factor is one of reality. Many of the plans that are arranged and the tasks undertaken in the higher realms during the sleep state have been worked out from a higher overall view of the events on Earth. It can be extremely confusing and make life and your interaction with others very difficult if you retain

this awareness of seeing what everyone needs to do in highest Divine order to bring about the successful conclusion to this plan. Because everyone has free will and choice, they don't always choose to follow Divine order. Also if you returned with your ability to see the thoughts and purpose of both the lower and higher selves, you may find it is not always easy to establish and define the border between the two. When one can see both, it is very easy to assume that the lower self is aware of the higher purpose. In that assumption, your words and actions could cause confusion, affect free will and possibly inhibit the growth of another.

As soon as you reach a point where you can retain a conscious awareness of all your night time activities and still operate in total clarity, focused and grounded, it will happen. The Earth Mission is on target and currently operating slightly ahead of schedule. There are times when it is slightly ahead or slightly behind, but a minimum base level is always maintained, thus ensuring a steady forward progress.

The majority of the Light Force, numbering millions, are now awakened and moving on their chosen path. Most are reaching the last stages of clearing their own third dimensional patterns. For the last few years, in addition to helping others, most have had a lot of attention on their own awakening and clearing – finding out why they are here and the nature of their own personal path. Many were looking for a specific role which they were meant to hold for the incarnation. Of these, many have since discovered that often this involves a sequence of different tasks and that all they need to do is to be in the moment and follow their excitement.

As one becomes more fully awakened, there is less interest in channelled material, books and workshops. One is then more likely to attend a workshop only because of a desire to share the energy and company of other lightworkers. The linking together of lightworkers and light centres across the world is moving at an incredibly fast pace. As was foreseen in the original plan, the increasing speed of communication is greatly assisting. Perhaps when all in the Light Force realise that they have the capability instantly to discern different energies and levels of truth, a system will develop that connects every light centre across the world, which is a possibility offered through computers.

With most of the self-preparation done, each light master turns his/her attention to their next phase of work. Many will feel excited about reaching out into all fields of humanity, spreading Love and Light and increasing vibration and awareness across the Earth. Whilst it may not always seem that the task you are doing is very spiritual, it is important simply to trust in the Divine process and the higher overall plan.

Much of Earth's population is already very spiritually aware, but it is not necessary for people to know of spiritual things. No-one needs to have heard of the concept of ascension in order to ascend. If it had been necessary to the success of the plan for every individual to become aware of all things spiritual, a longer period would have been needed to achieve the goal. What will be necessary for each is that they link to the Source. This can be reached by moving from fear to love. There are many parts to the plan, but sometimes something as simple as seeing someone who is very loving can cause an individual to decide to become more loving themselves. The Light Force around the world can show by example that life can be lived in loving harmony. Seeing this, many will choose this as a way of life for themselves.

Every individual makes choices of how they wish to live their life. If they choose to live in a negative way, they are choosing to remain in a third dimensional learning pattern. Anyone making a choice in any moment to think or practise in a negative way, disconnects from the Source. During moments of negativity, their personal vibration rate cannot be increased. Through excessive use of negative energy, it is possible for an individual to decrease their vibration back into a denser, slower energy. Remember that higher speed and lightness of vibration, permits greater connection to higher levels of truth and wisdom.

If they choose a positive loving route, they will automatically link to the Source. This connects them to the harmony and the natural movement of Earth. As Earth proceeds towards her new evolutionary position and her vibration continually becomes faster and finer, everyone who connects to the Divine universal flow then naturally connects to Earth's increasing vibrational rate.

This will happen in each moment that someone is connected to the Source.

Connecting to the movement of the Earth is not the only way an individual may ascend. Anyone can move quite independently of the Earth and raise their own vibration to one of pure Light. The Light Force are moving ahead of Earth, as they are creating a path for others. Through wisdom and love, anyone can ascend at any moment. It has always been so.

There is a great deal of joy and love present now on Earth. If we limit our perspective to the one generally portrayed by much of the media, we will perhaps see a focus on fear and suffering. Of course, it is we who choose the content of our media. The era ahead will be one of infinite joy. We are leaving behind a 'time is money' based society and moving to one based on love. Here it will be truly understood that **all** life forms are part of God and each must co-exist in harmony and peace.

Many major universal cycles are coming to a close and higher evolutionary opportunities will exist in many spheres. Our galaxy, with the Earth, is one of the major transformations now occurring. It has been ordained and it shall be so. It does not require that you believe this for it to occur. You already agreed to it long ago and it is the Divine Will of God.

The Earth Mission is nearing its completion. The dawning of the new age on Earth, the seventh universal Golden Age is now upon us. The entire galaxy now moves into the fifth dimension. A wonderful new world spans the horizon as the magnificent splendour of the gold ray of God permeates the consciousness of every man, woman and child on Earth, bringing recognition of the divinity that exists within all life. An old way of life is ending and a wonderful new world is beginning in a new dimension that incorporates the divine qualities of unconditional love, harmony, integrity, service and peaceful coexistence.

Earth is attaining sacred planet status, coming up from the deepest density ever experienced in the Universe, into a dimension of full Light. This will bring all pain and suffering to an end. All the learning that has been attained upon Earth now passes into the universal consciousness, creating a new pattern for the entire Universe.

Across the Universe millions watch in awe and excitement as this massive transformation takes place. Earth begins to emanate a violet hue and a great wall of Light extending beyond 100 miles becomes visible across galaxies. The entire galaxy now moves in unison with the Earth.

As the last energy grid patterns and blueprints are anchored into position, the Earth is in readiness for her final shift into a new dimension. The Rainbow Warriors, caretakers of Earth, now hand the sceptres to those who will guide the new millennium on Earth.

The amazing dedication of the Rainbow Warriors on Earth and the unswerving love and help from the ascended realms has brought this plan in all its perfection and glory into full reality as Earth moves steadily, positively and unfailingly into her new role in the fifth dimension.

CHAPTER TWO

The Original Agreements

E ach starseed and lightworker agreed to a series of incarnations, to become inhabitants and focus the Light to bring about a change in the balance of the Earth's energies. Almost all star-seeds and lightworkers were due to finish toward the end of the 1990s.

An overall plan was drawn up containing a myriad of functions, covering every area to ensure the freedom of every being and life form on Earth.

As each of the Light helpers chose the area they wished to work with, individual programmes were worked out and teams were formed. These teams came to Earth and the long programme began, with many becoming teachers, philosophers, helpers and carers of the Earth.

THE ORIGINAL AGREEMENTS
* I AM
* I AM INFINITE LOVE
* I AM TOTAL INTEGRITY
* I AM INFINITE AND INVINCIBLE
* I AM HERE IN SERVICE TO THE LIGHT
* I AM A CREATOR OF REALITY
* I AM EMPOWERED TO ACT IN THE NAME OF GOD
* I AM HERE TO ASSIST THE BIRTH OF EARTH INTO A NEW DIMENSION
* I AM HERE TO RELEASE ALL LIMITATION UPON THIS PLANET
* I AM HERE TO CHANNEL VAST QUANTITIES OF LIGHT ONTO THE EARTH PLANE
* I AM A MULTI-DIMENSIONAL MASTER, HAVING BORNE THE DENIALS AND LIMITATIONS OF THE EARTH PLANE, I NOW RELEASE ALL, TO ALLOW THE TRANSMUTATION AND TRANSFORMATION OF EARTH AND HER PEOPLE INTO THE GOLDEN AGE OF PEACE AND LOVE

🌿 I HAVE THE RIGHT TO REQUEST ASSISTANCE FROM THE GREAT
   FORCES OF LIGHT, ALL COUNCILS, ALLIANCES, FEDERATIONS,
   ASCENDED MASTERS AND EVERY KINGDOM ON EARTH
🌿 I HAVE THE RIGHT TO DECREE UNDER UNIVERSAL LAW
🌿 NOW IS THE TIME TO DETACH AS AGREED, TO FULFIL MY TASK
   AND RETURN HOME
🌿 ALL IS WELL AND IN ORDER IN THE UNIVERSE

The first six points being self-evident, the rest are now covered in
more depth.

I AM empowered to act in the name of God

Being here as a missionaire in Divine service (for which you are
fully qualified or you would not be here) you have the right to
access and use various energies, powers and abilities. These rights
become accessible when you reach a point where the ego has
blended sufficiently with Spirit. This is the stage where integrity
and your service role becomes foremost in your life. You will find
from that point that the abilities required for you to achieve your
tasks will be present as required. You do not have to struggle with
exercises and rituals to gain these abilities. If you simply follow the
Divine flow and discipline yourself to do this, everything unfolds
in perfect order. If any particular exercise feels right for you to do
and brings excitement, this is a sign to proceed with that.
Remember that there are a million different ways to attain abilities
and healing on this planet and the ways you personally chose long
ago will bring the pre-encoded feeling of excitement. You have the
Right to Decree (Chapter 9). You are co-creators bringing to Earth
the realisation of evolution into the fifth dimension. Through your
mighty 'I Am' presence, you have the authority to act as God.

I AM here to assist the birth of Earth into a new dimension.

The Earth is evolving from the third, through the fourth to the fifth
dimension and you are here to help it do so.

1. The **third** is the solid physical world we see around us. The
   entire visible world including our bodies, are a part of this
   dimension. In this dimension there is a time span, between
   when we think a thought and it manifesting into a reality in the
   physical world.

2. The **fourth** is the world of emotions. A fourth dimensional body containing all emotions, exists around every living thing including the Earth itself. If you can see auras around people, trees and animals, etc. you are viewing in the 4th dimension. This plane contains the apparency of time and one still uses **memory** in order to 'Know'. The lower part of this dimension contains the realm known as the astral plane.

3. The **fifth** is a world of Light, in which life is experienced through higher wisdom, love, peace and harmony, where everyone is aware that **all** life is connected. There is no duality in this plane. To be visible in this dimension one uses a 'light body'. Existing in the eternal **now**, there is no 'time' and therefore no karma. Because there is no time, **thoughts** are instantly manifested. This is the realm where one simply **knows** and no longer needs to create mental pictures or store thoughts in a memory bank, **in order** to 'know'. You are accessing the fifth dimension on those occasions when you 'just know' something. For example, if you are unable to see auras, but can simply know the aura colours, you would be using a fifth dimensional ability. It is a world where relationships in every form work in harmony and cooperation with each other. Beings living in a fifth dimensional world live in peace and joy, free of pain and suffering, co-creating new societies and technologies that work in the harmony and love of Divine order. Spiritual and psychic abilities, such as telepathy, are inherent to everyone in this dimension. There is no ego here to play out its many games of power, control and one-up-manship. Instead, all souls choosing to learn in this dimension enjoy the harmony and bliss of co-creating a new world and sharing loving relationships with every life form. All planets follow the same evolutionary pattern, evolving up through ever finer frequencies of light, as does everything in the entire Universe.

In order for the Divine plan on Earth to work, it was necessary for the starseeds to have the 'Veils of Maya' dropped. This means that it was necessary for them to forget who they truly are. The reasons for having to incarnate physically, and for then having to forget the plan were as follows:

1. In order to fully adopt the Earth patterns of limitation.
2. To truly become inhabitants of Earth.

3. To gain further learning whilst on Earth.
4. To make it easier to remain grounded in a third dimensional world. Also let's be honest, we all know that we wouldn't be too inclined to stay and experience any incidents of discomfort, if we realised we could leave and avoid it – this will make sense as you read on.
5. To bring the blueprints already manifest in the etheric realms, down into the solid form of the physical plane. An example of manifesting from one realm to another would be when we travel with our physical body to a specific location on Earth, in order to channel light into that area.

I AM here to channel vast quantities of Light onto the Earth plane.

The lightworkers on Earth have a great capacity to channel Light. Owing to their high evolutionary levels, the upper chakras (energy centres) of the body are capable of absorbing vast amounts of Light, depending on the ability and openness of the individual to receive. A person mainly using the lower denser chakra energies, as for example being obsessed with sex or food, would probably not be able to access great amounts of Light at that point.

The agreement you made was to channel Light using the additional chakras due to be re-opened at the time of the awakening. The Atlanteans used a twelve chakra system. The additional chakras were closed down after Atlantis sank, as they would not be needed until this decade. There are three faster energy chakras above the crown chakra, for connecting and channelling high frequencies of Light. There is one new one in the body structure, and another below the feet that is used to ground and balance the higher chakras. The plan was to access the higher frequencies of Light, allowing it to flow down **into the Earth,** as well as **out through your aura** thereby passing **into the aura of every person,** animal or living thing you come into contact with. They must be open and willing to receive it. They in turn would carry this Light to others who were open to receiving it. You do not need to be consciously aware of giving or receiving Light, as this process is done on a higher level than that of most people's conscious awareness. When you envisage many millions of lightworkers on Earth all passing Light to their entire surroundings and it then being passed on again and again, with millions of people and places being reached daily, the concept is magnificent. If you feel an urge to go to a certain place, trust it. You are probably responding to an inner knowing that you have an agreement to be in that area, or are required to carry Light into that area.

I AM here to release all limitation on the planet, and

I AM a multi-dimensional master............... into the Golden Age of peace and love.

The agreement was that the starseeds and lightworkers (with the exception of those who only began incarnating recently) would take on the limiting patterns of Earth. This meant in order to achieve the mission goal, each person had to incarnate here and take on all the various beliefs, fears, conditioning, thoughts, opinions, judgements, prejudices, attitudes and fixed patterns of the racial, national, educational, religious and social doctrines of Earth.

The plan stated that at the designated time during the last decade of this century (the end of the Piscean Age) the Light Force on Earth would awaken and begin releasing all these adopted patterns. **This would create an energetic pathway right across the planet to make it easier for the inhabitants of Earth to release their patterns also.** A partial analogy is that the first person to run a mile in four minutes, broke down a long standing mental barrier. This made it easier for those who followed to match it and strive to do it even faster.

The easy way to achieve this is to become your true Self. To do this, you **begin affirming you are a master.** As you affirm the reality of this truth, anything around you that is not in accordance with this reality will start to disappear, both in your life and in all your lower subtle bodies.

As you become more your true Self, your own Light begins to shine more brightly. You emanate a loving expression that can be perceived by others. As people see the love in you, they begin to make a conscious decision to be loving themselves and in so doing they link to their own higher Self and to the Source. If people cannot see that it is possible to live life in a balanced and loving way, it is hard to realise a life without pain and suffering. As people perceive this possibility, a spiritual recognition is triggered. The being becomes aware on another level, that it is possible to change their life from one of pain and suffering to one containing joy and love.

You need to **release all patterns up into the frequency of Light**. This can be done easily by just allowing everything to flow up into Light, without stopping, resisting or making judgements on the thoughts, emotions or situations that present themselves in your life.

The alternative and more difficult way to do this releasing, is actually to experience these buried thoughts, emotions, etc. viewing the details of how you acquired them in the first place. This could be a very long and tedious process and you could well find you would still be here at the end of the next century! If it feels right to review the details of a particular experience that is presenting itself, follow your own guidance.

You will have to release all fears, conditioning, attitudes, any barriers and walls you have created, all structures, expectations (that keep you from being in the present moment), judgements, control mechanisms, negative thoughts and feelings, fixed levels of consciousness that hold you back, all identities and beingnesses (mother, brother, boss, typist, a Christian, being 'good', being 'right') all planetary systems, regrets, prejudices, shame, national and racial beliefs, thoughts of being a victim, lack of responsibility, ideas of vulnerability, beliefs in duality (good/ evil, pleasure/ pain), the past, blame, serving others in **a victim or martyr role** and all dependencies you have created. This applies not only to this lifetime, but to any patterns you have carried through from past lifetimes. If you have had a particularly sad or painful period in a past incarnation, you may find that you were unwilling to view it at the end of that incarnation. It then remains buried and carried forward into other lifetimes. It will actually remain with you until such times as you view it or release its dense energy.

As the limiting patterns are released, you become more and more your true spiritual Self. As you release the dictates of the mind and move into the heart, you begin to operate in the Divine flow. This is letting go of 'my will' and moving into the selflessness of Thy Will. As this is done, the ego-incarnated soul identity begins to merge with its higher Christed Self. As the merge takes place, you begin to pick up your empowerment and move from the realms of suffering into those of joy and love.

They shall mount up with wings as Eagles. *(Isaiah 40:31)*

Of course, these patterns began clearing as soon as a lightworker became spiritually awakened in this incarnation, which for many could have been twenty, thirty or more years ago. However, the awakening that began in 1990 was to the memory of coming to Earth to serve. This triggered many specific programmes that you had stored in the higher dimensions to assist completion of your tasks. It was at this point, that a major clearing began **together,** as agreed, to create a **unified** bridge of Light for all mankind.

You may recall a previous lifetime, perhaps in Buddhism or a similar spiritual practice, where you felt that you achieved a great harmony and oneness with the Universe. Perhaps you felt you had found enlightenment and were free of the karmic wheel of endless births and deaths. You may also recall the shock of the following lifetime when you found yourself back in the third dimension in physical form again. The reason you returned was that you agreed to stay on Earth until the end of the mission. You also agreed to release your adopted Earth limiting patterning **in this decade.** Therefore, following your integrity for the highest Good, you took everything back 'on board' again.

One point to note here is that only a percentage of starseeds took on the **very** densest of these patterns. There are some bands of very dense energy on Earth and there are beings who have fallen into states of catatonia, robotism, believing they are matter, and so on. In order to give the possibility of freedom and choice to every being here, it was necessary that the **entire** spectrum of density was adopted. This ensured that the energetic pathway of Light began at a deep enough density to allow any beings located in these denser bands, to release their patterns and attain ascension also. To achieve this, meant that at some point during their incarnations, the starseeds who had agreed to help those in the lower densities had to experience the trauma of these levels. This was in order to incorporate the relevant patterns into their field. They must actually have these patterns within their field, before they can be released to allow the creation of a path of energy out of that density. This fact of taking patterns on in order to release them now, applies to almost everyone here who is helping to create an energy path.

Many beings have experienced trauma and suffering in order to bring this planet to its current position. However, everyone has also experienced great joy, love and many lifetimes of wonderment that left one breathless and filled with the awe and perfection of the divine nature of our Universe. Many new experiences and lessons have been gained toward a greater universal understanding. It is easy to forget all the wonder and bliss of our lives when we get caught up in the process of releasing uncomfortable experiences.

The great learning that has been achieved here in this heavy density will now pass into the consciousness of everyone in the universe. Never again will anyone need to learn through the depth of pain and suffering that has been experienced on Earth, for all will know and understand both its origin and its outcome.

I have the Right to request assistance from the great forces of Light, all councils, alliances, federations, Ascended Masters and every kingdom on Earth

You are able to request assistance, from either an individual or a collective energy of the higher realms. You may ask for assistance to help you carry out an action or you may request that this presence or energy undertakes the task. Provided the request has to do with a desire to bring something into closer connection with the Divine Source, this will receive attention. When you are operating **fully** in service, everything you do has a Divine purpose which would mean every request would qualify for added assistance. However, because the higher overall picture can always be seen from the upper realms, they may not act in the specific way we may see as most beneficial.

The crystals and stones of the mineral world have long awaited this time of opportunity to help and may be used to assist. Crystals are living and many have their own mission functions. If you choose a crystal **intuitively** to perform a certain task, you are unlikely to override the crystal's function. If you are not sure what that is, try a meditation. The crystal can easily speak to you, if you are receptive to its gentle energy. Quite a few Lemurian souls have incarnated into crystals this lifetime. Lemuria was the major continent prior to Atlantis. The race was very loving and its remnants can be found in the Polynesian races. The crystal energy is very close to the gentle loving Lemurian energy. If you have any crystals that you have perhaps stored away in a dark cupboard and forgotten about, perhaps this is a good time to bring them out and clean them. It may be a Lemurian! This will allow them to get on with their own long awaited mission functions. Remember it is important that all crystals are kept clean. This can be achieved by soaking them for twenty-four hours in water containing sea salt in a glass or china bowl. Put different types of crystals into separate bowls. You can also bury them in the Earth for the same period. There are various other methods. Remember that quartz crystals try very hard to remove all negative energies from your space. If they are not cleaned very regularly, they have to stay encased in this negative energy! As crystals may work with either light or dark energy, it is a good idea to choose them yourself or through friends who can sense these qualities.

The world of the little people – the fairies, pixies and all those who are part of nature, may also be called upon. These gentle creatures are so willing to help if treated with the gentle and subtle vibrations of energy that they are comfortable with. The fire salamanders, the water nymphs, the air sylphs and the earth elementals or nature spirits are all delighted to assist, and happy they are being asked to help. You may empower any of these to bring energy or healing into your life. Whilst having a bath or shower or swimming in the ocean, you can ask the water elementals to put healing qualities into the water. "In the Name of God, I empower you to bring healing qualities to this water". (Repeat this three times.)

I have the Right to Decree under universal law. (See Chapter 9, which is devoted to this important area.)

Now is the time to detach as agreed, to fulfil my task and return home.

You have agreed to detach emotionally and mentally from any dependence or need within the physical plane. This does not mean you become a robot or that you can't have any possessions. It means that you are to let go of any and all considerations and beliefs 'that you **need** something' other than just to be yourself, if you are to survive. Whilst you have been incarnating here, you have forgotten that you are a master and do not *actually* need anything. During your time here, you will have become used to forming mental image pictures and storing them in your memory. In truth you can just know and do not need pictures 'in order to know'. You may have created thoughts that say you **need** security, people, support, safety, sensation, food, a job, possessions, animals, comfort, children, a body, car, money, sleep, touch, time, solid objects and space. There are also needs that are a little less obvious hidden within our thoughts, such as – the need to be in control, to manipulate, to threaten in order to become more powerful ('wait till your father/ mother gets home'), remain healthy, or the need to look younger or older. In other words you need to detach from any ideas you have formed that say 'I must have it or I won't survive'. As you come more into service, a greater detachment from everything occurs. As the ego-incarnated soul identity blends with the 'I Am' presence, love becomes unconditional. It also changes from something that was a part of the lower spiritual, mental and emotional bodies into a very all-encompassing, deeply spiritual care and love for all life in the Universe. As you join the 'I Am' presence and detach, you will find you can more easily fulfil your mission tasks. When all the agreements you undertook are completed, you will go home.

All is well and in order in the Universe.

This key phrase is a trigger for the Light Force. It was designed to trigger a recognition within you that a major stage of the plan had been reached. It signifies a wonderful point planned so long ago, when the surplus **negative** energy on Earth would be replaced by a surplus **positive** energy throughout the entire structure. This has now occurred. When looking from a third dimensional viewpoint one still perceives negative energy, but the balance has changed. This planet is moving now into a dimension that does not contain duality or opposite polarities and therefore will have no negative energy.

Other key trigger phrases, such as 'The Time is Now' and 'It is Time', are also used to help awaken the starseeds and lightworkers.

'Now is the time' is used to help awaken the ETs and walk-ins. Technically many people could be classed as ETs. However, we refer here to the relatively few in number, out of the millions of Light Force workers that have come in to help from specific planets, mostly as 'walk-ins'. Sedona in Arizona is one of the major locations on Earth for this group. The techniques used to assist in the awakening and cleansing process for these beings contain their own specific planetary vibratory pattern. Because of this difference in vibration, these techniques are not meant for and cannot really assist the rest of the lightworker force. It is also possible that these techniques may cause some distress to those they are not meant for. It is up to each individual to follow their intuition regarding **any** clearing techniques they choose to undertake.

Specific terminology is being used more and more now to assist clarification for the lightworker. The word 'alien' is generally now used to refer to negative forces trying to thwart the plan on Earth, and ET for the friendly forces helping Earth. It may be a good idea in conversation with others to clearly establish definitions of these and other terms, to ensure no confusion arises.

ADDITIONAL AGREEMENTS **made by some of the starseeds and lightworkers:**

- **To manifest the universal blueprint of the new combination light body into third dimensional physicality by permitting the transmutation of the physical form of DNA's double helix carbon-based structure to a triangle silicone-based structure to a specific frequency of light.**
- **Should a mission team member be unable to carry out their agreed upon task or tasks, another may be called upon to handle this function.**

To manifest the Universal Blueprint of the new combination Light body, etc.

Those attaining ascension in past times, followed the only blueprint available, which allowed the physical body to die.

Having increased the vibration of the surrounding lower **subtle** bodies, they 'raised' themselves into the fifth dimension. There is now an opportunity to change this universal blueprint and ascend **all the lower bodies,** bringing a new pattern of ascension into **universal manifestation.** For the first time in the Universe, it is possible for those choosing it, to increase the vibratory rate of the molecular structure of the **physical body.** This means raising the vibration of the physical body to the frequency of Light. This means changing the DNA and RNA from a double helix, carbon-based body to a triangular patterned, silicone-based body. In order to manifest this blueprint, a specific minimum number of beings are required to go through this process. (See Chapter four). This process is available to everyone. First it needs to be done by the starseeds and lightworkers who are needed to help bring it into form. It is then immediately possible for every human being in the Universe. In the original agreement, a percentage of starseeds and lightworkers agreed to transmute their physical bodies. The plan however, allows for any and all members of the Light Force also to choose to help this blueprint become manifest.

Should a mission team member be unable to carry out their agreed task or tasks, etc.

An additional agreement taken on by some starseeds and lightworkers was that should any starseed choose not to awaken to his or her tasks, another would step in to handle them in addition to their own. The original arrangement was that each missionaire was either already an expert in their chosen field of help, or arrangements were made for the person to learn these skills during the incarnational period. This would ensure that they would be an expert by the time of the awakening. If another person has to suddenly step in and take up unfamiliar tasks they are not trained in, this can be quite difficult. A situation could arise that required taking on just the odd one or two tasks (sometimes with only a few minutes notice) or it could be a whole lifetime of extra tasks. When someone is called upon suddenly to perform a needed task, they have to do the best they can, until they can access the appropriate programme for this task. This is done through the 'I Am' presence.

Owing to the high level of evolution of the starseed, it was conceived that they would be able to function in the most dire of circumstances, should that ever be the case. Although generally it has all run quite smoothly, there are occasions where stand-ins are needed and this has required great stamina and focus of Light.

To sum up briefly why the Light Force came down into this density:

1. To greatly increase the Light on Earth, thereby changing the balance of energy from negative to positive. This would allow the planet and humanity to evolve into a new dimension.
2. To release the learning pattern of what has occurred on Earth into the universal consciousness so that this learning can pass to all beings in the Universe. This negated the possibility of anyone needing to learn in such a dense energy again.
3. To be the trailblazers, creating a path of Light energy, to allow humanity to release all their fixed patterns of limitation.
4. To manifest into physical form, the blueprint of the new combination physical/light body.
5. To further their own evolution by experiencing this solid density. Whilst all have experienced solid third density planets before, none had experienced the level of energy of this particular planet up to now.
6. To further their own evolution by undertaking to change the atomic structure of their own third dimensional physical human body to that of Light.
7. To bring to an end all pain and suffering in the galaxy. By bringing Earth into the new level of Light it would enable the entire galaxy to evolve into the fifth dimension.

It is occasionally written that the people here, including the lightworkers, were abandoned by the Light and are controlled by some other nasty planetary groups. It has been suggested that their memories were wiped, genetics tampered with and all manner of things. This theory offers that the people here are total victims, have had no control over their destiny and some suggest that we will have to forgive the Light Brotherhood for abandoning us and will need to make these other planetary groups answer for their crimes.

In any universe (there *are* others), many types of learning exist. Every lesson learned takes a being to greater love and wisdom. On occasion, planets have been at war, and throughout the course of history things have occurred that seemed 'unpleasant'. But never in the history of the Universe has any being had **no control over their own destiny.** Every step, every action, every relationship, every undertaking is agreed to by each individual. Occasionally an agreement was made through the group soul, the 'I Am' presence, or perhaps so long ago you've forgotten about it. There is no occasion where anyone can claim to be a victim or have had no hand in the creation of their life circumstances. There is never anyone else to blame. There are no accidents. We always choose. We are constantly making choices in every moment. We choose whether to follow our inner guidance or the dictates of the mind; we choose to trust or not, to be a master or a puppet, to love or not, to judge or not, to be still or chatter, to help or not, be involved or not, to discern or not, to be grounded, balanced or spaced out, to be disciplined, to think and act in a positive or a negative manner, to take the viewpoint of a creator or a victim, to move with integrity or deception, to live in truth or lies, to create harmony or discord, to be fearful or have courage, to be in one location or another, or to be with a certain person or not. Whether these things have occurred or not, is irrelevant. Your past does not determine your present. Everything that is with you now, you have created and are holding onto **in this moment.** Release all thoughts of blame. Be the creator you are and remember, you are working toward unconditional Love for everyone.

A common cleansing technique is to forgive everyone for the harm they have done to you. This is a positive step. It also assists to forgive yourself, for anything you feel you have done to yourself or others.

However, there is a stage further than this on the path to enlightenment. This is an awareness of a higher truth that there is nothing to forgive, because we totally create our own reality. This means that nothing can be done **to us,** because we attract or magnetise everything we experience in our world.

Another realisation is that we are all **one** and so everything we do, we are doing to ourselves. As one attains higher wisdom of these concepts, one also realises that only love, integrity, compassion and understanding, exist within the heart of God. It would be a lower ego statement and show a lack of higher spiritual understanding, for anyone to say 'well, if no-one is actually a victim and we are really all one and immortal, it is OK to do anything to anyone, because no-one can really be harmed'.

For all eternity, it will always be that each creates their own destiny.

If you search deep in your heart, you will find that you truly agreed to all that has occurred to you and that you were never abandoned by the higher realms of Light. There is no-one you must learn to forgive. The lightworkers and people of Earth are eternal, immortal, infinite and loving children of God. God abandons no-one.

CHAPTER THREE

The Pattern of Evolution and Learning on Earth

Evolution requires the soul to learn unconditional spiritual love. Each soul incarnates as many times as necessary into some level of energy. In order to obtain the learning and wisdom necessary, he/she plans out lifetimes to concentrate on specific spiritual qualities such as patience, humility, integrity, wisdom, power, hope, clarity, compassion, truth, gentleness, patience, thoughtfulness, kindness, harmony, respect, faith, peace, love, balance, forgiveness, understanding, dedication, devotion, purity, divine will, freedom, trust and love. As a being grows, becoming wiser and more loving, his own vibration becomes lighter and finer, allowing him or her to perceive higher and finer levels of existence (higher dimensions).

Each person has his/her own unique energy vibration which we are recognising when we feel someone is instantly familiar or feels comfortable. Whilst each being always holds this special energy, their overall vibrational field alters depending on the current level of evolution he or she is at. Their vibrational band determines the world he or she sees. All dimensions exist in the **now**, but we can only see things that lie within the vibrational band of Light that we resonate with – that matches us. Wisdom and love raise one's vibration, taking it from dense, slower moving frequencies to faster, finer frequencies.

The Earth was once a perfect ball of evenly distributed energy. She agreed to share a learning process with humanity, and so began the pattern of learning through **limitation.** The experience of this learning has caused an uneven distribution of this energy, through the use of negative thought. This pattern has been taken to its greatest learning potential and could be considered to be complete.

Earth agreed to this joint learning with man and had a deep understanding of the various possibilities that could occur. She operates from a place of love and does not feel anger about the apparent destruction of her form. Everything in the Universe is done by agreement – everything. She watches with love and perceives the struggle within humanity to overcome all the barriers they have set themselves.

Everyone on Earth is special and unique. Each has his own role to play in the overall scheme of things. If each follows what he feels right to say or do, then he/she will be carrying out their part in that plan. If instead, you permit yourself to do that which you 'should do', often through guilt, you are liable to be stepping outside of your agreements.

It is time to 'Let Go and Let God'. This is truly taking responsibility. To achieve this requires patience. The modern world promises us instant results; credit, fame, wealth, entertainment, relief from colds and pain and instant communication through satellite, faxes, mobile phones and computers. We are not used to waiting and often become impatient when we have to wait in queues and traffic lights. In order to 'let go and let God', we need to bring a stillness into our life and be willing to wait patiently, allowing each moment to unfold according to Divine order. This would mean not taking things into our own hands, but trusting in each moment that we will feel what is best highest order. Trust, delight in God's will, commit yourself to Spirit, be still and be patient. *(Psalms of David, 37)*.

As you make this connection as a spiritual being, follow your heart and feeling of rightness, without hesitation. If it feels right for you to help the dolphins, save the rain forests, increase awareness of child abuse, or do nothing – the range is endless – this is part of your agreement. However, because this is right for you, it does not have to mean that it is also right for others. Each has his own task to do, and if you permit yourself to be talked into what you 'should be doing', you will not be able to carry out what you are really meant to be doing in that moment. If you do what feels right in the heart, from a place of love and not from fear or guilt, then you can trust that you are in the Divine flow. From that place you can intuitively sense the next move.

It is time for everyone on this planet to make a choice about the sort of world they wish to live in. One of peace and love – or the world we see now upon the Earth.

In the current third dimensional reality on Earth, one learns compassion, understanding and love through experiencing every conceivable situation in life, ranging from poverty and struggle to wealth and power. This involves learning to rise above the limitations set by ourselves prior to the incarnation, thereby gaining strength and wisdom. Finally, as you cease to judge and realise that 'I am my brother's keeper' and that in truth, every form of life is a brother – you can move to a place of peace and unconditional love.

Much of humanity now feels that they have learned sufficiently in this realm and would choose to release the various patterns belonging to limiting learning and move on up to higher levels of learning. Learning goes on through higher dimensions, but it is through greater harmony and less solid types of experience. Whilst joy and peace *can* be found in the third dimension, they are a matter of course on the higher dimensions.

Everyone is now making a choice. As the planetary vibrations continue to increase, all old rigid structures and systems across the Earth either change their basis of operation to one of love, or they crumble and cease to be. All buried thought and emotion is being released individually – nationally, internationally and planetarily. All remaining karma is being balanced out across the face of the Earth and everyone who chooses love is light-ening up as their vibration moves into higher frequencies.

It is time to step free of fears and the myriad of belief patterns that keep us so boxed in a world of structure and control; time to move forward in trust and faith knowing there are worlds beyond what we can see with our eyes.

Planet Earth offers learning through limitation. This means that one limits oneself and then grows in wisdom and strength by rising above the barriers that are put up. Humanity has excelled in this by taking limitation to its extreme. Millions of limiting patterns have been introduced into society. Man now no longer has any idea that he creates his own reality and his world, or that he is a child of God, connected to everyone and everything. He limits himself with ideas – such as one needs money, food, water or shelter in order to survive. A predominant pattern on Earth involves the vulnerability of the body – like beliefs that you can get ill if you eat the wrong food, drink too much alcohol, have too much cold, heat or rain – as well as a long standing deeply-entrenched belief that the body has to die. The process of learning through limitation can occur because there is a time period between thinking a thought and the moment it manifests in physical form. This means that by the time something happens, you have forgotten that you thought it.

Let us look at the classic example of a limiting pattern. It is generally considered that one should date or marry within one's own background, education, social and financial position, nationality (or even local community), race, religion, age group, and not with a close family relation. There are also conventions about the right 'looks', weight, height, physique, eye and hair colour! Quite restrictive, isn't it?

As for learning on Earth, you will find that if you remained aware that you are truly spirit, you wouldn't really gain a full learning from your experiences. This applies to the entire spectrum of learning while incarnate. Agreements and plans that are made with other team members prior to incarnating are usually forgotten around the time of the baby's birth. This applies to every being incarnating on Earth, including the mission team. The only exceptions to this are some of the recent walk-ins who often retain a knowledge of their identity and purpose here.

Let us look at why it wouldn't work if we remembered our pre-incarnational planning. Let's say that you sat around the planning table in the realm of Spirit, making your agreements with a partner with whom you had chosen to share some learning experiences in the lifetime being planned. This will often be with someone you have had a close relationship with many times before.

As you review previous incarnations, looking at the areas where you did not love others unconditionally, you may see that you have a pattern of walking out on relationships. It seems as though you have little understanding or compassion of what it actually feels like when a loved one leaves. You also see that there is another area for growth for you – in having to experience the handling and overcoming of the various difficulties of a single parent in raising small children alone. Deciding to incorporate these two learning areas into the next incarnation, you plan with your partner to meet up at specific time, fall in love, marry and have two children. You arrange that when these children are aged 18 months and 3 years old, your husband will leave you for another woman. The financial situation is set up so that there will be hardship for you to overcome. Incidentally, both the children and the 'other woman' are sitting in on this planning meeting, interjecting details of what they require for their higher growth. So are all the other beings who are to play a role in this lifetime, such as your family and friends. Understand that the planning is quite intricate, as each of the team members is planning out their own goals and growth requirements as well.

Sometimes there is a waiting period involved if a team member is not yet available. It may be that a person is already incarnate, but won't actually be needed to enter as a player in your incarnation, until perhaps your fiftieth year. They may be due to 'die' out of their present incarnation several years before that. Allowing for the period of time they will need afterwards to review the lifetime they have just left, they can agree to take a part in your incarnation. The agreements are conducted through the higher Self.

Then you incarnate and everything happens according to plan (it doesn't always go as originally planned, as you always have 'free will and choice' to change direction). The children are now at the right age for you to leave your partner. Can you see what would happen at this point if you were aware of the plan? You would be looking at your watch and saying to your husband something like "Isn't it about time you left?" You had planned on gaining spiritual strength from overcoming the trauma and hardships from this apparently unknown and unexpected experience in your life. How much do you think you would gain if you knew what was to happen?

When you begin your first incarnation in a third dimensional world, such as Earth, its requirements are very general. It doesn't really matter what religion, nationality or social class you are, because you haven't experienced any of them yet. The main requirement at this stage is that you are not involved in a situation that is too demanding or where you would need a good understanding of third dimensional life in order to survive. A simple role is usually planned, involving a loving situation, perhaps where teamwork is important, rather than individual survival. An example of this might be incarnating as a mentally retarded child who is capable of giving and receiving much love, without anything being demanded from him, or perhaps a child in a peaceful native tribe, residing far from the 'civilised' world.

As you continue along this evolutionary path, each successive incarnation requires greater planning, because there are fewer situations left to experience. The last few incarnations of life in a physical realm require a massive amount of intricate planning. They need to include the balancing of all karmic energies and work on all spiritual qualities not yet perfected, which may include integrity, harmony, love, truth, wisdom, honour, peace, compassion, devotion, purity, freedom and courage.

Everyone's life has an *overall* purpose, with additional smaller goals within. When that purpose is achieved (or entirely abandoned), the incarnation is complete. The goal of a lifetime does not have to be anything grand or be spiritual. It could be absolutely anything in the early stages with goals such as to learn how to function using a human body; to live with nature; to succeed at something; to experience a relationship with the opposite sex; to be a contributing member of a team, and so on. This would lead up to larger goals in the final incarnations such as: to be in communication with the gentler subtle energies of the deva kingdom; experiencing the totality of the elemental world; to experience absolute Oneness with the Universe, or to give to Earth in selfless service to God.

The final incarnation requires a very intricate plan, needing specific beings to play co-creative parts. All areas must be balanced out in the last incarnation. Of course, if the last remaining lessons are not learned or the various energies are not brought into balance, then another incarnation on some planet will have to be arranged.

For the mission team on Earth, the situation is somewhat different. The vast majority had already completed their last incarnation in a third dimensional world prior to coming to Earth on this mission. However since coming here, they have experienced further incarnations, with their usual ebbs and flows which need to be brought back into balance and released, even though they were deliberately taken on.

In the later incarnations, one recognises the simplicity of life and begins to live in the Divine flow. By the end of the last incarnation in physical form, an understanding has come of one's Divine nature and one comes into a state of peace and joy. From this wisdom, the illusionary world of the third dimension is accepted with humility and gratitude for the gift of learning that has been given. Now the next dimension begins to become more real than the third.

Looking over the whole learning process, we eventually begin to realise that we are all connected, like brother and sister, to all life forms. We see that the different races, nationalities, customs, life-styles, beliefs and religions bring a great richness to life in a third dimensional world. One can use the analogy of a salad. We could look at the wonderful qualities of the red tomatoes, green lettuce, orange carrots, purple beetroot and yellow sweetcorn, each bringing its own unique colour, vitamins, minerals, texture and flavour, to make the whole complete. We each follow a different path, learning in our own way in order to bring that wisdom back to the whole. There are millions of different ways to do things. There are many different paths to discover, many healing methods and various ways to experience life. Each of these ways is a form of learning and experience and none of them is a 'right' or a 'wrong' way to live our life, but simply one we have chosen to experience. In this place of wisdom, we can allow everyone his choice without judging the rightness of that choice. **If there was only one way to do something there would only need to be one person.**

Parallel Universes are brought about by thought. Here we can create alternatives and variations to life. We create 'reality' by our thinking. This means that the full spectrum of the way life is lived is created by each individual, both in their own personal life and for the planet as a whole.

On an individual basis, whatever you most believe will occur, does occur. On a national basis, the same thing applies. What the majority of people believe is most likely to occur within a specific country, will become the reality that will be lived by the people in that country. People not holding that belief pattern will find that whatever is occurring, including the circumstances involved with it, doesn't really play a part in their lives.

If a certain number of people believe a certain reality for Earth, that creates one possible future for her future. If a number of other people believe a different set of circumstances will happen for Earth, that creates another possible future, and so on. All these realities as to the future of Earth exist at the same time. A term that is often given to this is 'probable reality'. All the different realities are in a state of creation, but the one we are **living** is the one that the majority have agreed is the most likely 'probable' reality. Should the 'balance of power' shift, which would mean more people start believing in one of these other possibilities, then we would begin to live that reality. Without addressing accurate figures, let us say five million people believe that we will probably have a Third World War on Earth. Ten million believe we have learned our lessons from wars, and that from now on the world will remain at peace, believing that any difficult situations will be resolved with peace talks. What is being created here is 'No Third World War', because the majority are choosing to experience peace. Incidentally, the possibility of a nuclear war was decided against by everyone on Earth on a spiritual level, about twelve years ago.

We have seen many prophecies of great destruction on Earth and talk of huge land masses sinking. Realities that seemed the 'most probable' when viewed by Nostradamus and more recently by Edgar Cayce, have since altered and are no longer probable contenders for the future of Earth. Owing to the tremendous work done by the lightworkers on Earth and the ascended realms of Light, a great change in mass consciousness is occurring.

A great responsibility lies in the hands of the lightworker. It is the power of positive thought. If you agree that the Earth needs to be cleansed in a devastating and traumatic way, then you are adding power to this creation with every utterance and every thought. Every time you tell someone that this is what will happen and they decide to believe it, their energy is also added to this creation. If instead, you see that the Earth may be cleansed gently and easily by being filled with Light, you add power and energy to this reality. Every time you pass on this information to others, more and more energy is added to this reality. The first scenario creating fear, sees people moving inland and storing food supplies.

The second reality creates love, positive energy and finds people forming light centres and visualising Light flooding the Earth. There is absolutely no doubt that it is we who decide exactly what will happen to Earth.

The most probable current reality for Earth, by far outweighing any other, is the ascension of Earth **in a gentle way**. The likelihood of this changing is extremely low, as it has been already been agreed by the Light Force.

The most probable current reality of how that will occur will be the one the Earth Mother herself has chosen and is backed by the majority. The choice she has already made is that it will occur gently with the minimum of disturbance. She wishes to use the Light being sent to her to transmute any dense energies that may still be contained within her. She has the same physical, emotional, mental and lower spiritual body as we have.

To the degree that the lightworkers continue to create this as a reality and do not agree with scenarios that would predict mass death and destruction and the amount of light they continue to focus, will be exactly how gently the Earth will make her ascension. The whole process could take place without one flood or Earth tremor. This is not to imply that one reality is wrong and another is right, simply that alternatives are available, and we choose which one we wish to create.

It is entirely up to the responsibility of the lightworkers fully to grasp beyond any doubt the idea that **'You Create Your Own Reality'**.

Another concept that needs to be quickly grasped is the great power of thought. In fact, just about the only true area of difficulty left on Earth that a percentage of the Light Force still haven't truly understood is that each time they think a negative thought, they are creating it. Also, each negative thought places a little hole or tear in one's auric field which can let in negative energies or entities. As each lightworker connects more fully with their 'I Am' presence, the power of their thought magnifies greatly. When fully operating with the I Am, there can be no negative thought at all. Everyone is therefore being shown in his or her life how fast and effectively their thoughts are working. The gap between the time you think a thought and observing its manifestation in the physical Universe, is lessening. This is so that everyone can get used to the idea of being a master operating with positive creation. You as the master can choose a positive reality for Earth.

Perhaps you would prefer to choose the reality that the Earth IS a perfect balanced, harmonious world of great tolerance, peace and love, receiving a continual flow of love and Light from everyone on Earth and in the Heavens. This uninterrupted pure flow of the Love and Light of God is gently permeating through every life form on Earth, all dense energies having vanished into pure Light.

CHAPTER FOUR

Ascension and the Birth into a New Dimension

Ascension is a natural and normal part of the evolutionary process of the Universe. It has always been so and will probably continue until it is no longer necessary as a universal process. Ascension is a stage in evolution that involves reaching a place where one is ready to raise oneself to the frequency of Light, whereby the fifth dimension then becomes accessible and visible.

When the real meaning of the concept of **ascension** is grasped, one realises it is not a new process – not something for the 'chosen few', but available to every being in the entire Universe. It is obtained on an individual basis, within the time frame that a being chooses to experience his or her growth. It is inevitably gained by everyone at some point or another.

One does not need to understand the process or to have ever heard the word in order to ascend. It is simply a word that is used by some to define this particular step of one's growth. All stages of evolution are wonder-full and contain their own special beauty and wisdom. However, many feel that ascension is a special stage as it involves the transition from a third dimensional reality of duality and its relevant learning, to an awareness of oneness, harmony and love.

The planet we know as Earth has reached the point in her evolution where she has chosen to increase her vibration rate to a level we call Light. The process of changing the vibration to reach this level of light and the fifth dimension is called ascending. All planets in the Universe attain ascension and now it is our Earth that is doing so.

There is a being who has the planet Earth (it has other names, such as 'Terra') as her solid body, just as humans have a solid form. Usually it is the inhabitants of a planet who are ready for and initiate this step of ascension. In this case it is the **planet** that has chosen to ascend, thus giving all her life forms the opportunity of ascending with her. Everything has been planned and those on Earth now are able to tune into this assistance.

As the entire planet moves into finer frequencies of Light, every individual on Earth has to choose whether they wish to align with Earth as we now approach the new millennium. This will be the Golden Age of peace and love, predicted by so many philosophies and religions for so long, shown on the ancient Mayan calendar and known deep within the heart of many, many millions working in the Light of God.

Every life form that is linked to and identifies with the Earth's natural energy will automatically make the changes in frequency, because they are operating in harmony with it. This will include most of the living world of insects, plants, trees, birds, animals, water and minerals.

The exceptions are humans or evolved animals who are consciously able to choose whether or not they wish to link to the Earth. This would cover a proportion of mankind and animals who have evolved beyond the 'group soul' level and so are able to make individual choices in their lives. This would apply to any developed life form which operates with individual will (my will). To the degree that one is using 'my will' as a priority, one is separated from the Divine flow (Thy Will). Perhaps you are wondering what happens to isolated peoples of Earth who may not be able to receive spiritual information. Many of the tribes, in less so called 'civilised' countries, already have an awareness of Divine law and live in complete harmony with nature.

Dolphins and whales are highly evolved 'old souls' from the Sirius constellation and are not therefore classed as animals. From the perspective of other civilisations in our Universe, the Earth has two intelligent species, the dolphin/whale and the human. The dolphins and whales have remained on Earth from Atlantean times in order to help at this special time. They bring great joy and healing to those who connect with them. The dolphins have many diversified functions here now. Their current tasks involve reflecting the qualities of love, joy and fun for humanity to perceive, bringing awareness of the connection and love between human and animal, communicating to starchildren babies, assisting fisherman and people lost at sea, healing sick children and directing the space fleets to areas of the ocean that need help.

The whales are the libraries of Earth. Those people who find the urge (and the courage!) to swim with these massive whales, will find that information has been passed to them. Both these species are completing their last physical incarnations now. This united decision was made by the entire dolphin and whale population in 1990. Some of them are choosing ways to die that will bring human attention to the connection they share with us and to teach humanity that all life is precious. If you feel that part of your work here is saving the dolphins and bringing awareness of their plight to human consciousness, then this would also be part of the overall plan.

Each being on and within the Earth structure – and her entire energy field, including the surrounding fourth dimension and astral plane (lower fourth), whether incarnated or not – is now being offered an individual choice. This is whether they wish to move into the divine flow and link to Earth's ascension to the harmony, love and oneness of the fifth dimension or whether they wish to stay in a third dimensional reality. Those choosing the latter would continue to learn to balance and ultimately rise above the concepts of duality, materialism and all aspects of limitation. Anyone choosing this would need to leave Earth and do so on another third dimensional planet outside this galaxy. This is because all planets in this galaxy will be in the fifth dimension or above, so there will be no third or fourth dimension here.

Any person who decides to continue their third dimensional learning will be assisted by their guides and angels to another planet in this dimension. There is a planet just outside the edge of our galaxy that looks similar to Earth and it is expected that any person wishing to continue this level of learning will probably go there. There are also other third dimensional planets available in various galaxies. Perhaps everyone on Earth will choose fifth dimensional learning!

As the planetary ascension takes place, its vibration or energy gets increasingly finer and faster. A person making a choice to remain in a third dimension effectively prevents their own vibration increasing from its current density. Most of those choosing this pattern will reach a point where they are too uncomfortable living in the planet's increased finer vibration and their bodies will 'die'.

If, somehow, anyone did manage to tolerate the vibrational changes and is still on Earth at the time she shifts to her new dimension, it may be possible for them to be relocated with their physical body to another planet. Although the idea may be a little difficult for some people to grasp, it is possible to relocate people. Not only that, but it is also possible to move people in their bodies without them realising that anything in their life has changed. This ensures they do not become traumatised through suddenly finding the world around them is completely different.

This is similar to the process of forgetting what the Light Force and humanity have experienced during the normal process of incarnation. The situation in which these people find themselves will be acceptable to them and all the pieces will fit. The fact that the majority of the Earth population, including probably some of their friends and family, are no longer present, will be acceptable to them. It is similar to when you are a baby; it was acceptable to you that your abilities were limited and you had to learn to walk and talk. In truth, you have many abilities and you can probably speak many planetary languages!

The karmic requirement for completion of third dimensional learning on this new planet or any third dimensional planet these people may go to, will be the normal requirement under Universal law. This is because the new planet will not have the negative imbalance that allowed the special dispensation of 51% that was given to Earth (see Chapter 6). They will proceed with the same lessons they were learning before the changeover took place and will carry with them the same level of karmic balance they had already reached prior to leaving Earth. They will take with them whatever negative energies are in their field when they leave here. You may wonder why these could not be removed, to help them reach spiritual attainment more quickly on their new planet. If this were done for them, the opportunity for them to see the effect of these energies would be denied.

Also, people choosing further third dimensional learning will no longer have the added influence of the Dark Lords. These were responsible for the imbalance of the Earth energies (albeit with the agreement of humanity's negative thought patterns). It has been ordained by God that the Dark Lords are to be returned to the Light. They have gone beyond the point of being able to conceive that they are in truth, children of God. Through their constant negativity, consuming need for power and the build up of the ego, their connection to the Source – the threefold flame of God has become so blackened that no Light may enter. Their free movement in the Universe is over. They are to be returned close to the heart of God – to strip away their negativity, thus allowing a re-connection to the Source. They will then start their evolutionary path from the beginning again. This time they will have within themselves an understanding of what occurs when an individual works solely with negative energy, moving from the Divine path of God. This same knowledge will be passed to everyone through universal consciousness. The actions of the Dark Lords, if viewed from a higher perspective, have presented a great learning to this Universe.

In order to ascend, the planet and each person choosing ascension needs to bring the density or frequency of the four lower subtle bodies (physical, emotional, mental and lower spiritual) up to that of Light. There are eight subtle bodies and four are termed 'lower'. This means that any part of those lower bodies that contains dense energy, has to have that energy raised and released. The types of situations that usually have dense energy attached to them are upsets, traumatic experiences, unhappy thoughts, pain or anything 'in the dark'. We do not need to pay attention to the four higher subtle bodies.

All that is required for any life form to ascend is that they link in to the Divine flow of the Universe. They need to permit any dense vibrations around them to come to the surface and be raised in frequency which releases them.

There is a choice in how one raises these energies up to the surface. The tough way to do it is to attract into your life the necessary situations and people that will trigger these things. For example, you may have had past traumatic experiences of losing loved ones and the pain of this has been buried deep within the mind. You may then attract into your life a situation in which someone you love leaves you. This will have the effect of triggering the earlier painful experiences and you will find that you are handling this old pain as well as the current one. This is often very difficult as it is all much more intensified. It does however, handle this buried energy (providing you do release it and don't bury it back down again!). If you bury it again, you will then have to attract another set of circumstances into your life to help raise it up again. If you continually do this, life can become pretty uncomfortable.

The easier and more graceful way to do this releasing, is to increase the intake of Light by becoming more one's true Self. This can be achieved via many routes, including affirming a new reality of Self; letting go of the controlling structures of the mind; meditating, visualising flooding oneself with Love and Light and allowing ego to blend into Spirit and service.

It is time for an attitude of 'out with the old and in with the new'. Have a clear-out and change all those things that are not in harmony or are truly representative of **the you that you are Now.** This means every area of your life; the colours and styles of clothes you wear, the furniture, pictures, wall colours and decorations in your home, friends, job, way of life, all your fixed patterns and comfort zones – anything that is not reflecting the vibration you are now. Review your Christmas card list, your shoe rack, music, the dark cupboard, attic, old papers, clutter and things you keep in case they may 'come in handy'. Realise also that you are continually changing, so this will need constantly reviewing.

We complain about the quality of our 'throw away' society that gives us modern furniture, clothing, cars, fashion trends and electrical goods and objects that don't last very long. You often hear people say 'they don't make them like they used to'. Furniture was made to last, shoes and clothing were made of natural fibres and were easily repaired, parts for electrical goods were easily available and it was usual to replace the part rather than buy a new item, and generally things stayed around much longer. However, as we know there is always a higher purpose to be seen and the apparent poorer quality and service of modern day life, forces us to constantly renew the energies around us. We are in a new time and this time demands that we keep the energies around us matching the constantly increasing vibration of both the Earth and ourselves. With the current system, we are more likely to have around us things that are created **now.** The latest technology, new ideas, new timber, minerals and materials – all these things contain the new finer energy vibrations. Surrounding ourselves with new finer energy, rather than older, denser energy assists us greatly in our progress toward ascension.

As you increase your own vibration, you will feel more comfortable with things around you that are of a similar frequency to you. You will feel tranquil and at ease with the areas of similar vibration and uncomfortable with colours, objects and people that are not similar to you in vibration.

This doesn't mean you have to follow current fashion or even that you need money to make these changes. You simply create the space to allow the new to present itself. You may be given all manner of things, if you permit the abundance of the Universe to reach you. Recognise who you are now and fully support that reality in your life. It is amazing how many different ways the universe has of presenting its abundance, if you will only allow it. If you keep your life clogged up with old, dense, vibrations that are no longer relevant, you will stop whoever or whatever is meant to be in that space, because it can't get in.

If you don't quickly spot the lessons to be learned in life, the same thing occurs. Then you will have a continuing pattern of attracting the same type of person and the same sort of situation into your life, over and over again. The new people and experiences that are really meant to be in your life cannot come in, because you are not ready for them yet. It can make life very stagnant and repetitious, instead of fast-moving fun, with increasing awareness and wisdom. You can actually feel the rewards of a fast pace in your life. When you are spotting quickly the lessons to be learnt, you feel the excitement of winning and realise you are swiftly progressing.

The Earth has similar choices to you in how she does her clearing. She can raise the frequency of her bodies gracefully, by absorbing greater Light, or she can do it through geophysical changes, such as earthquakes and floods.

The Earth has to bring all the energy within her structure back into the perfect ball of energy it originally was and raise the frequency, in order to make her ascension. The Earth Being is quite capable of doing this. The way she does it, is dependent on the amount of Light she receives. She wants to release these areas as gently as possible, and we are assisting this by focusing Light in and across the Earth, creating positive and healing patterns around the world. Prayer also has always been a form of connection to the Divine Source of all, and we know this links to the power of God. Using The Right to Decree, assists greatly.

Another way to assist the Earth is by keeping our own auric field (aura) clear and free of negativity. We can then allow Light to pass through the energy centres (chakras) of the body, down into the Earth. You can keep this field clear through the discipline of permitting only positive thought, pure intent, using affirmations, being non-judgmental, moving from the 'head to the heart', realising that everyone is connected and becoming more loving. There are various products available that assist in raising vibration and help to clear the lower bodies. There are colour, sound, healing oils and crystal essences or the high vibrational combination bottles, such as Avatara Harmony (Vicky Wall's niece) and Aura Light, for these purposes. When considering any of these, use only what resonates **in the moment** and feels right for you. Products that may have been highly effective in the past, may no longer be pure or contain the vibrations necessary to assist us or the Earth. Each of us has different needs, and whereas one may find that aromatherapy produces miracles, someone else may need more peace in their life or to look at the area of confidence or self love. There are many paths because people are different, with as many different needs. By following our intuition we can lead ourselves to increased awareness and higher levels of evolution.

For many people, it feels right to help the Earth in a more practical way. This is also helping greatly. If it feels right for you, trust it. She is very grateful for all forms of help. When sufficient Light is brought in to help this transmutation, the Earth does not then need to correct the energy imbalance in a geophysical way, such as through earthquakes, floods, etc.

In her love and compassion for all life upon Earth and for her own comfort, she would naturally prefer to have a pain and trauma-free transition. As we know, most mothers would choose the gentlest birth possible. She is no exception and doesn't enjoy the pain of cracks and upheavals in her structure, or the added trauma of human suffering.

This is where the special dispensation of energy from the hierarchy (see Chapter 6) and the tremendous work of focusing Light by the incarnated Light Force, greatly assist Earth. To the degree that Light is received in by Earth, so can she transmute gracefully. We can also use the wonderful gift of the violet ray, given to us by St. Germain, its chohan or guardian. The violet ray is a high frequency vibration and transmutes all lower density energies. When one is releasing negativity in any situation, access the violet ray and visualise violet pouring through that thought, place or person. This transmutes it to a higher frequency becoming positive energy. Negative energy doesn't just disappear, it moves out and hits someone, somewhere, unless it is transmuted. Violet is the colour of the highest frequency energy chakra in the body – the crown chakra.

Everything now on the planet that has its basis in a dense frequency – meaning anything fixed and immovable based on old ideas, concepts, lies, power, control, fear and materialism – has to free itself up and begin moving with the increasing planetary frequency. If it cannot or will not shift its rigidity, it will simply crumble and disappear. What is required now is a movement into Spirit, bringing with it ingredients such as love, compassion, tolerance, truth, harmony and balance. We see many things changing now, such as the ending of communism, the demolition overnight of the Berlin Wall, the collapsing of major insurance companies and banks, the advent of women priests, the re-unification of South Africa and the election of Nelson Mandela as president, the end of the Cold War, great changes in the traditions of the Royal Family and the movement toward peace in Israel and Ireland. Permanent peace will be achieved when the people of each nation demand it. Many situations present now on Earth will be resolved when the individual, the community, the nation or indeed humanity, take their power back.

All these things are a move from individuality to Oneness. However to achieve this, each individual must now resume responsibility for the creation of his or her own world. It is very much a part of current practice to be constantly handing one's power over to councils, governments, doctors, police and various people that we think must know better than we do. We believe that we are victims of circumstance. We do this out of fear and a feeling that we can't manage our own life. All power now must come back to the individual. Now everyone must realise that they hold the Light and potential within of becoming a Christed being. In truth everyone is already this and needs only to know it is so. We create our own reality. The Oneness being attained is a recognition of our inherent Divine connection to all life. Do not confuse this with the third dimensional 'One World Government' plan to control the population.

This rule of becoming self-empowered also applies to gurus and philosophers, past and present, who have played a large part in the evolution of this planet. Now the ones of Light are telling the people that there is no need to seek outside themselves for God, for this connection lies within each one. Spurning adoration from others, they are handing back the power to the individual. Through the divine use of God's Will, everyone in the Universe has the right and the power to manifest and heal.

There are no leaders or authorities bringing in the new age on Earth. Millions of people are involved, each seeking the truth within themselves rather than from an outside authority. All are becoming masters and seeking their own connection to the purity of God/ All-that-Is/ the Source. This is the perfection of the Divine plan on Earth.

All serving the Light are assisting and encouraging each other to take up their own power. There is no one guru holding sole power for anything. Everyone is sharing in anchoring the new energies, such as the feminine principle, now reaching Earth. There is nothing in the Divine plan for Earth that tells us that only one person will ever be allowed to channel the Ascended Masters or cosmic beings or have access to highest Truth. There is no one person or one group who hold the sole rights to the ascended realms. There is no elite or select group solely graced by God. Look in your hearts. Would any of these things ever truly be so? Also, no-one is born of evil and warrants expulsion from your heart. The wondrous gift of Love we have been given is for all mankind, for everyone is truly a child of God. If you perceive energy you would prefer not to work with, that is discernment. If you then say that this is a bad energy and withdraw your love, this is judgement. In so doing, you have failed to see the higher picture and have denied someone their right to learn and evolve.

We have the use of many wonderful tools now to assist our healing, such as crystals, angels, guides, healing oils, flower essences, etc. It is wonderful to be able to use these things, but recognise also that we have these same gifts and power, within us all, through God's 'I Am' presence.

It is predicted that hospitals will continue to close down as the responsibility of healing moves back into the hands of the individual. It will eventually be realised that Spirit is the true creator of illness and that it is the **thoughts** that precipitate all illness, mental and physical. The **common cold** for example, is always caused by a loss. It is a manifestation **created by the being to fill the void or space left by a loss in their life.** This can be an actual loss or an anticipated loss, that perhaps never happens. The moment of loss is the **thought** of the contemplation of loss, that **precedes** the actual event or possibility thereof. Of course, what constitutes a loss differs with people. To 'cure' a cold requires only that you locate and view the moment of loss. This observation only applies to someone who has a cold and no other symptoms. A good source of the type of thought patterns that cause specific illnesses can be found in the A to Z at the back of the book *You Can Heal your Life* by Louise L. Hay.

A great awakening and a new consciousness is taking place across the world. We are all aware of great changes on Earth. We are also receiving special signs that are intended to remind us who we are. Many lightworkers are being offered unusual and wonderful rainbows as a sign of their Divine connection. People have seen upside down, triangular and multiple rainbows. The rainbow has a great significance and it is said in the Bible that God set it in the sky as a promise that never again would the Earth be devastated. Many people have seen dove-shaped clouds and the Archangel Michael's sword Excalibur.

During this awakening, a total balancing is taking place. As we become informed about the various planetary suppressions, we also receive a greater awareness of natural Divine law. Both are being brought into view, to be absorbed and digested. If you are not viewing the information about planetary suppression from a high enough perspective, you can easily fall into the third dimension trap of thinking that it is all bad. Understand that the things you read and hear of have been occurring for a long time, but have been kept hidden. Now they are all rising to the surface to be seen, so that people can accept responsibility and decide what they do not want to happen anymore. People are becoming more aware of the condition of the world, as the suppressed information is released.

We discover global warming, the repercussions of felling huge areas of rain forests, the poor treatment of old people, the massive use of chemicals in our food and water, the poor quality of care for the disabled, the corruption of politicians, the abuse of children, the side effects of prescribed drugs. Then there are the depletion of the ozone layer, the effects of pollution, the cruelty of animal testing for medicines and cosmetics, the antibiotics and chemicals fed to sheep and cattle to stimulate growth, sewage polluting the oceans, the treatment of animals by abattoirs, young calves taken from their mother after birth, the tactics of major business with dishonest practices, manufacturers suppressing inventions which will affect their profits. Lastly we learn about the conspiracy of a one world government, countries secretly staging wars and the control of the world by a few wealthy families.

At the same time we are also becoming aware of thousands of new forms of natural healing. Osteopathy, chiropractic, aromatherapy, colour therapy and reflexology are just a few of the natural methods now used in many hospitals in the UK. People are beginning to accept possibilities of life that hitherto would have been instantly dismissed, like reincarnation, acupuncture, vitamin and mineral supplements, health food, vegetarianism, telepathy, ghosts, the benefits of swimming with the dolphins, a sixth sense and even UFOs. If we can release our fear of being viewed as cranks if we mention our interest in these areas, you may be very surprised at the dramatic shift in human consciousness that has already taken place.

There is also a new freedom of expression and much more tolerance, acceptance and understanding of others. Things that used to be swept under the carpet and kept very hidden such as mental illness, sex, homosexuality, children born out of wedlock, sexual abuse and racially mixed marriages, are now commonly discussed on major television shows.

This new consciousness is taking Earth and her people to ascension. People across the world are beginning to open more and more to unconditional Love. As people accept love, higher spiritual truths can enter and the fixed denser energies begin to release. This enables our awareness to increase and the vibration to quicken.

It has been difficult for some of the Light Force to experience love, because of closed heart chakras. Many Atlanteans closed down their heart chakras when Atlantis sank, the loss was so great. It is only now that some of these people are bringing this pain to the surface and opening to love once more.

A new light body blueprint has been brought to Earth. In the past, ascension has been achieved by an individual raising his personal vibration and his surrounding subtle bodies to the frequency of Light. The normal pattern was to allow the physical body to 'die' and increase the vibration of the subtle bodies. This allowed one to 'raise' oneself into the fifth dimension.

There is now an opportunity to change this universal pattern and ascend with all our lower bodies, bringing a new pattern of ascension into universal manifestation. For the first time in this Universe, there is a possibility for those choosing it to increase the vibratory rate of the molecular structure of the physical body. As in all new things presented to humanity, the idea may well seem 'way out' and impossible.

Ascension may now be achieved, including the physical body. This body, now raised in vibration to the frequency of Light would be combined with the existing light body, to form a new combination light body for use in the fifth dimension. This action brings into physical manifestation the blueprint that has previously only been present in the higher realms. This will allow anyone who reaches a stage of ascension in their evolution in the future, anywhere in the Universe, to be able to use this procedure instead of having to 'die' to achieve it. This would also apply to the current inhabitants of Earth so that for the first time there will be a choice of how one ascends. It also means that after this is achieved, by simply decreasing one's vibration to a lower density, one can instantly manifest a body in the third dimension. Thus no-one from higher levels would have to incarnate or 'materialise' in order to visit a third dimensional planet.

People attaining their ascension for the first time are forming their light body as they clear their lower bodies of the denser energies. The majority of the Light Force having previously attained their light body, simply bring it in from its 'storage' place in the fifth dimension. Regardless of whether one is retrieving or newly forming their light body, both may proceed with this new opportunity of achieving *a new combination light body.*

As one increases the light of the physical body, there are physical manifestations that accompany this change in body DNA. The most common are energy shifts that feel like bursts of heat through the body. These happen regardless of sex or age and are similar to the hot flushes of the female menopause. There is no special pattern to this energy. They could be very irregular, such as several a day for a few weeks, and then none for a while. This occurs as one makes adjustments to the change in DNA.

Another common symptom is of suddenly having difficulties with focusing your eyes, sending many off to the optician for reading glasses. One day your eyesight is perfect and the next minute you are holding the page further away in order to see it clearly. This is focus change which comes about because the incarnated soul is merging with their 'I Am' presence. This can take some time to complete, so you may find that reading glasses of the lowest magnification are the answer. There may be other ways to handle it. If you would like to check this, just request that your 'I Am' presence leaves your space for a few minutes. Your eyesight should return briefly to its previous condition.

Another symptom is a pitched sound or noise in the ears (not the same as the condition called Tinnitus) which is often a signal sent to your conscious awareness, reminding you to tune in on a higher dimension for an update. Occasionally there is a temporary numbing of a body part which doesn't usually last too long (happens to a small percentage of people). Many experience tingling, pressure or occasional headaches in the third eye and crown chakra (pineal and pituitary gland changes), influenza (a clearing procedure) and unusual aches and pains. These symptoms occur in all age groups and to both sexes.

Perhaps you have also noticed that you can't seem to get as much done in a day, as you used to. The reason for this is that time is accelerating as the planetary vibration speeds up. Although the clocks may appear to look the same, we have currently lost 6 hours, 25 minutes and 3 seconds (as at 12 August 1999) in a twenty-four hour period. That leaves us with a 17 hours, 35 minute day. This pattern of 'losing time' has been occurring now for several years and the momentum is quickening. This will continue until there is 'no time' left as we move into the eternal 'now' of the fifth dimension.

You are probably also experiencing blank spots through your day, when you suddenly realise that you were 'off somewhere'. This is your adjustment to becoming multi-dimensional during your conscious waking time. Blank spots can occur for another reason. Often words can disappear in mid sentence when you are saying something that is pure truth.

Many council meetings take place in different sectors and locations during the night, as plans are reviewed and changed to keep in step with the speed of change occurring on Earth. Sometimes you attend as many as three meetings in a night. The higher realms are packed with missionaries attending these meetings. You can't find a parking space anywhere and the amount of coffee and cigarettes ... (joke!). If you tend to feel tired or worn out when you wake up, you can request from your 'I Am' presence that your agenda be shortened. This will ensure that you are not quite so active at night. These meetings are also the reason you are waking up at 3am and 5am – it is the time the meetings end. Yes, there is **time** involved. How would it be if you arrived back at 11am in the middle of the office!

Of course, there can be other reasons for waking up feeling exhausted. Someone complained of this happening and looked for the reason. It was seen that just as she was a curious person during the day, she followed the same pattern at night. She was rushing around, looking in on all the gatherings and council meetings, afraid she might miss something. When this was brought to her conscious attention, she made a decision to stop doing it and immediately the problem resolved.

If you are waking up throughout the night, it is best to gently accept this, without resisting, protesting or allowing yourself to fully wake up. This will allow you to go back to sleep again easily. Wise sages tell us to simply allow everything to flow freely, creating no resistance and therefore no blockages. There is a saying 'That which you resist, you may become'.

Occasionally, if you wake suddenly and come back into the body too quickly the lower bodies or auric field become unevenly balanced. You will find that if you can move back out of the body (or visualise it) and then gently re-enter, this should handle the discomfort. If you have difficulty with any process that requires visualisation, you can also **think** the words of the action, e.g. "I am now moving out of my body".

As this planet increases in vibration and moves steadily toward the fifth dimension, she is transiting through the fourth. This dimension is the realm of the emotional body, both for her and everyone on Earth. As this movement takes place, there is more and more cleansing, as different levels of emotions are brought to the surface and released. This occurs on individual, national, international and planetary levels.

If you live in balance between Heaven and Earth, you are then present in the 'now'. From being 'present' and grounded, you can more easily perceive what feels right to say or do in any given moment. This is Spirit. It comes spontaneously from the heart (Divine action, not reaction) and will contain interest or excitement, or simply feel right. It will lead you step by step along your path. You are always being shown your next right step in every moment and if you are moving in the Divine flow (Spirit) you will see it. Every moment is a choice and if you choose to move into thoughts or emotions that will cloud the clarity of Spirit, you miss opportunities being presented to you to further your growth.

You are being helped along this path by everyone you meet and by many angelic presences. Trust that your teachers, guides, angels and your 'I Am' presence are helping to place the people and situations in front of you who are designed to assist you. You will need to remain in the 'now' to see these opportunities. If you lack discipline and do not keep yourself in the Divine flow and in the vibration of Spirit, you could miss the chances. You would then need to wait until the circumstances can be arranged by your higher Self, to present you with another opportunity to learn lessons or allow abundance in your life.

To stay alert and grounded may require some changes in your life. The following steps may be of some use:

1. You may need to get more or less sleep.
2. Eat higher vibrational foods that are 'live', such as fresh fruit and vegetables. Avoid 'dead' processed food. Drink good

quality water in sufficient quantity. Avoid fluoridated and chlorinated tap water by using a top quality filter.

3. Do the type of work or exercises that assist grounding, such as gardening or other physical work.

4. Throw out everything in your life that you do not like or enjoy (sounds like a dream come true, doesn't it?)

5. Get out of any soul-destroying job. You will have to trust in universal abundance sometime, why not now?

6. Maintain a pure intent and integrity.

7. Cancel any negative thoughts as they arise. Words have power and the word 'cancel' actually cancels. Be aware of your negative thoughts. Handle them by keeping your attention to some degree on the thought and think 'cancel'. Fill any void or spaces you may have created when doing this by flooding the area with white light. This helps keep your aura clean.

8. Use the violet flame to transmute dense energies around you. Visualise the colour violet, flowing through any negative area or dense energy. This also helps keep the aura clean.

9. Don't allow yourself to wallow in criticism and judgement.

10. Maintain an absolute viewpoint of unconditional love for all life.

11. Concentrate on your breath. This is the one thing that is always in the 'now'. This is your link to the breath of God. As you put your attention on your breath, release your conscious control of it and allow your 'I Am' presence/Divine consciousness to take over. Your breath will usually change, often becoming gentler and slower. It is being adjusted into harmony with the Divine universal breath.

Each of us learns in our way, at our own pace. Look at the example of a mother's unconditional love, as she observes her young child's early attempts to clean the floor or wash up. Could you not adopt this same viewpoint? Does it have to mean that just because the people around you are now called adults and a bit older, that we have to expect them to act a certain way? Just because they no longer fit our definition of a child, do we need to become impatient and judgmental, because we've decided they 'should know better by now'? Who said they 'should'? What belief pattern does that fit into? Can we not grant them the right that we would wish others to extend to us. Most of us learned the rule **'Do as you would be done by'** in school – or did we? Surely we would all appreciate patience and tolerance from other people as we do our learning and growing. Just because something seems simple or obvious to us, it may not seem so to the other person. You are probably very capable and proficient in many areas, but remember that you also have had to learn.

These things are not difficult to do. It is a matter of overcoming our fixed patterns of behaviour and opening the floodgates to fun, joy, happiness and love.

The Three Waves of Ascension

A few years ago some channelled material was presented to the Light Force on Earth, mainly as audio tapes from the USA by Eric Klein. These channellings talked of three waves of ascension. It says clearly in the first few tapes that this was to be a new part of the plan. The first five of these channelled tapes from the Ascended Masters were badly recorded and difficult to hear. This may have been because this information was unexpected and time was needed technically to set up to record clearly. These crackling tapes found their way around the world, copied again and again. These wonderful words were listened to by individuals and groups across the world. The quality didn't seem to matter as the excitement grew and a great awakening took place.

You will recall that the **original** plan states that each missionaire will ascend **when** their individual mission is completed, and this plan remains. This channelling offering three waves of ascension, introduced a new concept into the original plan. This said that if individual lightworkers could clear enough of the dense energies in their lower subtle bodies, they could be assisted to a higher frequency of light, attaining ascension. The offer included assistance with raising the physical body as well as the other lower body forms. Although not given in terms of percentage, in order for a lightworker to be in a position to handle the incredible change involved in this shift (even allowing for the fact that they may well have done this before) they needed to have already reached a minimum 60% clearance of their lower bodies in order to be assisted. Universal law requires that they also needed to have already completed about 60% of their mission, but in the main this was already achieved. The proposal was that those who reached this stage of clearing could be 'lifted' up into one of the light spaceships of the Ashtar Command. This is one of the space fleets serving Earth. Commander Ashtar and some other commanders have impostors operating in lower dimensions claiming to be them (see note on False Hierarchy, Chapter 10). Whilst on the ships, the lightworker could become re-familiarised with their higher level abilities. It was estimated that this adjustment would take from several days up to a couple of weeks. It was hoped that anyone choosing this opportunity would be willing to return to Earth to complete their mission, as a master with full abilities. Those choosing this option could be placed back on Earth, either in the same family and location or, if it suited them, they could be placed anywhere on the planet where they could best serve. It was said that it was possible for those who wanted to go back to the same location on Earth to return in the 'same moment in time' of their departure. This could happen, even though they may have been on board the ships for several weeks. It was made clear that children, pets or anyone that one was responsible for, would be taken on board at the same moment. It was said that if a lightworker chose not to return to the same location, but wished to serve elsewhere on the planet, there were ways to inform their immediate family that they were all right. This was in order to prevent distress.

There were three waves of energy permitted by Divine dispensation, that were to be used to assist this to occur. As an act of grace, these waves would allow anyone who was ready, to be assisted to completion of their ascension. The timing of these was unknown and no dates were given. There were two reasons for this. One was the nature of free will and choice of the Light Force, which can alter everything. The other was that this dispensation was coming from a higher source than the realms of the Ascended Masters who were bringing forth the channelled information. The Ascended Masters said that, whilst they felt that the first wave was not far off, their concept of time differed from ours.

It was suggested that it would mainly be starseeds that would go on the first wave, plus any Light Force that could handle the initial

DNA changes. Many people really did very well and a great deal of change took place.

As the months went by and the first wave still hadn't been announced, the ability of some to maintain their spiritual viewpoint, remain enthusiastic and stay focused on the Light (all part of the testing) began to waver a little. Some people kept dropping back into old third density patterns, causing dense energy to shift back in around them again. The staying power and discipline involved to achieve the cleansing required a lot of faith and trust. Some people did some of the cleansing work and then sat back to wait, believing that the rest was all going to be done for them. Others accepted lower level channellings and negative intervention, encouraging them to starve themselves in order to purify their bodies. Although many of the Light Force very much wanted to go on this programme, some found it difficult to hang onto the discipline of constantly releasing their negative thoughts, confusions, judgements and third dimensional belief patterns, to meet the required percentage of clearing needed to carry out this programme. Many failed to discern the differing energies involved in channelled material and by believing 'everything', allowed confusion to enter their world. All these various thought patterns affect your ability to connect to the Source and Divine flow, which is necessary if you want to raise your vibrations into very high levels. It is not difficult to do these things, but after being incarnate in this density for a long time, it can certainly take a bit of getting used to acting as Spirit again!

Unless one has reached a certain level, the shock of a higher dimensional shift of reality can be quite traumatic, even fatal, to the physical form.

To attain mastership really needs the discipline to stop the creation of negative patterns. Negative thoughts need to be cancelled and transmuted immediately, because they affect all your energies and auric field. Discernment and intuition need to be used. One also needs discipline, to ensure one doesn't drop back into third dimensional reality, and to avoid wallowing in judgements, emotions or thoughts of what 'should' and 'must' be done. These things rule much of our lives and pull us from our inherent spiritual intuition and guidance. One may see someone who is very keen to ascend and who wants to serve humanity, who does a lot of clearing and cleansing exercises and then picks up a newspaper and in the next minute they are in a discussion with a friend about 'how terrible it all is'. They have abandoned a spiritual perspective and have decided to view this situation from a third dimensional reality. One can maintain a spiritual viewpoint and still feel a great love and compassion, without having to buy into the very limited perspective of the third dimension. In order to see the greater picture, simply come into the heart. Thus viewed, all becomes visible in the pure perfection that it truly is. If you cannot see the Divine perfection in any situation, you haven't looked high enough.

Some people held the focus and the discipline required. However, it was seen from the higher realms that it was not going to be possible for the mass physical ascension that had been proposed, transmuting the physical body. So the first wave physical ascension was changed to a spiritual ascension.

Even though not enough clearing had been done to allow a physical ascension, a major awakening and increase in awareness and vibration had occurred among the Light Force. Because of this major step forward, there was a unanimous decision made by the 'I Am' presence and the incarnated starseed. This was that it would be more beneficial to individual evolution not to use the assistance of the light ship (which initially had been offered to assist a **physical** ascension), but simply to use the assistance, whilst remaining on Earth, of the special waves of energy offered. There were just a few exceptions.

The first wave occurred through May of 1994 and those people who had held their focus of Light and cleared their lower bodies of dense energy to the degree needed, attained their spiritual ascension. This would have included a tremendous feeling of lightness and fineness. Most would remain aware they had attained a spiritual ascension from the benefits and abilities obtained. This could be withheld or withdrawn if there was any evidence that the person was dropping back into negative thought forms. Anyone using the power of God needs to be in a place of spirit and very positive in their thought and actions. However, once the state is attained, it is not lost, even if it appears to be.

Spiritual ascension could be called the first stage ascension. It is here one makes a conscious union with the 'I Am' presence and adopts the light body. From here the assimilation and adjustment to operating with the light body takes place and new higher abilities become apparent, as the 'I Am' merges more and more with you. If your discipline remains intact and the intuition is followed, you may find you want to eat only lighter foods and you will have lots of energy. If you continue clearing, remain committed to the process and are one of those who wish to transmute the physical body into Light, you may find that your full ascension could take place on the second wave. Also understand that no-one ever needs to wait for a wave in order to ascend. Any individual can ascend, whenever they have reached a space that permits this to occur. It has always been so.

Some lightworkers felt let down about the first wave and were quick to blame the ascended realms for the changes to the ascension waves, but in truth it was the lightworkers in combination with their 'I Am' presences, who made the changes. Free will and choice are great gifts and often produce quite different realities from those anticipated as the most 'probable' occurrence. Ascension will never be something that is done to you. It is a causative process of self-mastery. Don't get into a panic about these waves. They are only one option. Trust in Divine order that you will be in the right place at the right time. The original plan allows for your ascension.

A Summary

The overall and **original** Divine plan states that each missionaire will attain their ascension upon **completion** of their mission. That is the original agreement; it will always remain so and will apply to everyone following the path of Initiation (see Chapter 6).

Permitted within this plan, some will have chosen this special dispensation of three waves to attain an early ascension. At this point they can choose to return to Earth for the brief time it would take to complete their mission task. They may choose to return home, in which case another lightworker would need to complete their task.

The three waves of ascension plan is **an addition** to the main plan. It was interjected by the Hierarchy as a possibility to further assist the overall plan. Although it has since altered, it remains intact. This dispensation helps those who would like to ascend at a point **earlier** than completion of their mission. This option may be chosen by lightworkers wishing to complete the last stages of their mission in a more effective way. It is more likely that one would be ready for this, if the desire to help was foremost and not from a desire to 'get out'!

The Light Force on Earth has altered the offer of the dispensation of the three waves of ascension in two ways:

1. Very few will now use the assistance of being 'lifted up' by the space fleets, but will themselves directly access the waves of energy whilst remaining in their bodies on Earth.
2. Currently the three waves of the ascension plan are a spiritual and not a physical ascension. This may change for the second and third waves. Physical ascension will only occur to those who have agreed to transmute the DNA structure of the physical body. This will be regardless of whether they use the special three waves dispensation or choose to remain with the original agreement. Not everyone has chosen the physical ascension method. Some have chosen the 'normal' old route to ascend, through increasing the Light of the other three lower bodies and allowing the physical body to 'die'.

Note: Prior to the Eric Klein tapes which contained information of the new plan for the first, second and third waves, these terms had been used in connection with other occurrences. The first wave originally meant the 'old souls' or the first creation, and the second wave was used to define those who came later to Earth and were not 'old souls'.

Another use of the term first wave referred to the existing Light Force on Earth who were handing the sceptres over to those who would be incarnating in the new dimensional period on Earth (referred to as the second wavers).

There will be a smaller population on Earth in the new millennium, as there will be a greater choice of planets available for fifth dimensional learning. In addition to Earth, other planets offering fifth dimensional learning will now be more accessible. Virtually the entire Light Force will be leaving, as they are no longer needed here.

The Evacuation Plan

Owing to the free will and choice of the Light Force, many options were originally woven into the original plan to allow for different possible outcomes. Entirely separate from the new three waves of ascension plan, there has always been an evacuation plan. This allowed for the possible lifting by the space fleets of the entire Light Force and masses of humanity to a safe zone. This was to be implemented in the event that the Light Force on Earth chose to create the reality that the Earth needed massive geophysical cleansing. Whilst this plan will always remain as a possible option, it has been deemed unlikely for some time now that it would ever be put into use.

The Photon Belt

The Photon Belt is a large area of Light energy that exists in the Universe. It is composed of a combination of particles and anti-particles (such as an electron and a positron) colliding with each other. This disc-like sphere extends hundreds of light years into space and it takes about two thousand years for a planet to move though it. Although it contains no heat, it is a beautiful, powerful source of energy. It can affect all the molecules it comes in contact with, raising the vibrational energy. When anything with a level of vibration close to that of this environment enters it, its energy will be further refined, thus assisting its evolution. No darkness can exist where there is photon energy, either physically or spiritually. Prior to full entry of this belt, (which is still only a possibility), there could be a few days of darkness in a point known as the null zone. There is no need to be frightened of the possibility of a few days of darkness. In the polar regions this is experienced regularly. The Divine plan allows for it.

The planet Earth and the Photon Belt are moving gradually and gently toward each other. This event is eagerly awaited as a wonderful assistance to Earth in her evolution. This information was known to the Light Force prior to coming to Earth, as well as to those in the higher realms.

The Divine plan for Earth took into account the possibility that Earth may be receiving photon energy from perhaps the 1960s and that at some point may fully enter the Photon Belt. Although the timing was and is still unknown, it was conceivable that this would occur not long before the year 2011. As anticipated, the photon energy did begin reaching Earth in the early 1960s and assisted the Hippie movement's focus on love and peace.

The Mission plan is to increase the levels of Light on Earth and to raise human consciousness and vibration by the end of this decade. This ensures that Earth's population would gently move with her, and be ready as she completed her last movement into full Light.

Based on the effectiveness of the intricate Mission plan, it was considered that the Earth and all her life forms had the potential of already being **fully** raised in vibration, prior to the full photon energy reaching Earth.

The timing of the entire plan has been meticulously arranged. The preparations had to be exact to give the people of Earth enough time to make their link to the Source and raise their vibration sufficiently, to make an easy bridging into the fifth dimension.

It was originally planned that by the time the photon energy fully reached Earth, humanity would at least need to be close to the vibration needed for their ascension. They could then be assisted in the last stage by this wonderful mass of photon Light.

Let us look at whether we feel that humanity is at a level **now** to incorporate a mass of high frequency photon energy. We are seeing the Divine plan at work in the wonderful massive shift in consciousness that is occurring across the world. Everything is on schedule and the goals are being achieved. However, energy forces must be handled with care, or a shattering effect ensues. If you check with your inner guidance, you may perhaps feel that humanity is not quite ready for a sudden massive influx of extremely high frequency energy.

If the Light Force should decide that they want the Photon Belt to reach Earth before the bulk of humanity is sufficiently raised in vibration to receive it, it would seem likely that fear, chaos and mass death would ensue. Because the power would be similar to being struck by a bolt of lightning if beings were unable to cope with such a massive change, their physical bodies would die. The Light Force agreeing (**believing it will happen is the creation of agreement**) that Earth will make an early connection with the

Photon Belt, would mean that the bulk of humanity would not have the benefit of the many plans designed to increase awareness and vibration due to take place in this last decade. It would then follow that the majority could not attain ascension, but would need to continue in a third dimensional learning pattern on another planet.

The Divine plan for Earth includes the opportunity for all humanity to ascend and allows for each individual to choose this or not. Many long incarnations have been spent here by the Light Force to help this occur. The Light Force on Earth may consider it to be the highest wisdom to allow the Divine plan to manifest as originally laid out. We can make a personal decision based on our inherent spiritual intuition and heartfelt knowing. If you are unsure as to what exactly is the highest Divine order, you can use The Right to Decree (Chapter 9) and ask for whatever is best in the highest Divine order to take place.

Predictions exist to show us the current range of 'probable realities' that are being chosen by the majority as the most likely possibilities. This then allows everyone a chance of recognising that this is what is being created, so they can decide if that creation is acceptable or not.

Some predictions are complete fabrications, given out in the hope that they will be believed and so gain lots of agreement and energy, thereby increasing the possibility of that prediction coming true. Some predictions are issued as tests, others are made to allow us to see what we are tending to create. Some are channelled from beings in lower dimensions who are therefore not receiving an overall higher picture.

When a prediction is made that appears not to be in accordance with highest Divine order (often producing fear), this does not mean this event is a forgone conclusion. If anyone, upon hearing or reading such a prediction immediately believes it to be so, they have just added the weight of their own power and energy to that as a possible occurrence. As you realise that you create the world you live in, you start to take more responsibility about the things you choose to believe. You start to support only the highest truth.

Instead, when hearing such a prediction, you could act as a master and use your intuition to discern whether this 'possible reality' would be the most loving and optimum solution for the highest good. If you felt that this prediction would not be beneficial to the greater number, you could then make a decision to agree to something you felt would be best.

We create our own reality. The decision made by the majority of lightworkers, creates the reality that is to be experienced on Earth. Let us all continue to create the Divine plan on Earth in all its perfect magnificence.

A wonderful new world dawns on the horizon, bathed in the splendour of the gold ray of the Christ Consciousness, as we who choose it, come home.

CHAPTER FIVE

You Create Your Own Reality

T he truth of this statement is so outrageous an idea that it tends to be one of the last concepts in our life that we accept. As seekers of truth we have heard the term, but perhaps it is possible to take it to a deeper level of understanding.

Everything you see, feel, experience, perceive or are aware of can only be in your life because **you believe it to exist.** Everyone experiences a different world according to his/her belief patterns. If you do not believe it exists, it doesn't – in your world.

Your Thoughts Create Your World

Somewhere, somehow, sometime, you agreed that it was possible to see, feel, experience or perceive in some form, all the events and people who have been or are currently a part of your life.

Unbelievable as it may seem:
Every situation exists because you created it.
Every person is there because you attracted them into your life.
Every action you encounter, everything that happens to you or is done to you, occurs because you choose it.

If it is in your world, somewhere along the line you have conceived of that possibility. If you had not agreed to accept it as a possibility that could exist in your world, it cannot occur.

Belief patterns can be formed prior to birth whilst still in the womb and are also carried through from our previous incarnations. We often adopt the beliefs of our friends, family, the media, society and education. Some beliefs are passed on from generation to generation, such as the belief that the human form has to die, or that it is rare for someone to live to be a hundred. Actually, prior to the time of Atlantis, people on Earth may have lived for about 400 years. There are many beliefs found within each race, culture or nationality and whole systems of beliefs can develop or change completely within one generation. When you arrange your incarnations, you choose specific cultures to be born into and you are aware of the beliefs that already exist in those areas. You choose whether to believe these things or not. All beliefs, no matter how they are formed or where they come from, are agreed to by you. Additionally, no matter how they were formed, they actually exist with you in **this** moment.

Even if you had a belief pattern that you have since changed your mind about, you have already made a decision that it exists in your world. Even when we change our mind, we don't often completely relinquish and erase a belief. We usually still feel it is a part of the world we live in. Most of the time, we just replace one belief with another.

The belief that we have the most faith in is the one that is most predominant in our world. Whilst you may not have consciously thought about it in terms of a percentage, out of different beliefs you hold, the ones you *most* believe in are the ones that will manifest more strongly in your world. Let us say you have formed a 60% belief pattern from reading statistics, that 'two out of three marriages end in divorce'. You accepted this as your reality. It has now become your truth. You have created the possibility of experiencing this in your world. In addition to this, you have a 40% belief pattern that your own marriage will survive. In which outcome have you placed the most faith? Which one are you creating as 'most likely to occur'? Divorce, here we come!

You may say, "But those are the actual statistics, so they are true!" They may well be the current statistics. That doesn't mean you have to accept that reality into your world. It is someone else's creation, it doesn't have to be yours. Everyone is creating scenarios for their world. Each of us is choosing the world we experience.

Patterns are accepted into a society as a reality because people agree to them. Let us look at how something like this starts up. Perhaps a couple have a belief that their relationship will not last and consequently get divorced. Out of millions of happy marriages, one divorce occurs. This couple tell other people that they got divorced. It is unusual, so it gets talked about. People are curious and it spreads. Some people who hear of this decide it could happen to themselves or their friends. They begin mentioning this possibility to others. As more people pass this on, it gains more and more acceptance. It begins to happen more frequently. It starts to appear in magazines and television programs and gains further acceptance. More people are now creating this possibility in their world until, lo and behold, one day we hear a statistic that tells us 'two out of three marriages end in divorce'.

Everything in your world is the world you decided to agree to. Everything is there for you to learn about greater levels of love. The entire content of your life stems from two areas. Firstly, those things that you arrange prior to and during the incarnation for your highest learning. The second area covers the things in your life that are there simply because you agreed that it was possible for them to be there. They provide lessons, like the realisation that you attracted something because you believed it could be experienced in this world. You could then decide if you want to continue believing in that or you prefer to un-create it and let it go. There is learning to be gained from all experience.

If you decided to make a list of your belief patterns, you may be surprised to discover how many you have. As an exercise, try writing down your thoughts, opinions, feelings, considerations and judgements about the 'weather', including concepts of cold, hot, rain, snow, etc. If we looked at a subject like 'relationships', we may be writing for a long time. There are thousands of different aspects to our lives, all containing belief patterns. Each time you speak or think, you will be presented with your own belief patterns. The quickest way to release unwanted beliefs is to be in the 'now' and decide to let go of everything you do not wish to continue creating.

It has been part of our learning on Earth to have denied that we create our own reality. In order to learn in the third dimension (our world), you forget that you are a creator of reality. This is actually a necessary part of that learning, because when you acknowledge that you created something, it disappears. As a creator of reality, when you view something in total truth, which includes the fact that you created it, it ceases to exist. As soon as you view a truth, it is duplicated in its exact space and time and ceases to be created. Therefore in order to learn in the solid dimension on Earth, you lie to yourself and say 'I did not create this'. This then allows you to keep on experiencing a situation until you have learned its lesson. When you say 'I created this', and you know this to be true, the situation disappears. However, as evolution brings with it wisdom and the realisation that we create our own reality, this allows us to move on from the learning of this world.

We have a tendency to believe many of the things we read or hear. As you begin to realise that you create the world you live in, you start to take more responsibility for the things you choose to believe. You see that much of the world is caught up in a myriad of belief patterns, and perhaps you see some fixed ideas in your own life. You begin to 'free up' the rigid patterns with which you have structured your life. This allows more freedom to reject or accept concepts that you hear or read. You start to accept only the highest truth into your life. You may decide to see it from the viewpoint of a creator of reality. Instead of reading something, automatically giving it credence and believing that is how it is, you may choose to say "Is this reality the highest wisdom for everyone concerned?" "Is this a reality I choose to support and add my power and energy to?" Perhaps you feel there is another reality that would be more beneficial for everyone concerned. If you feel unsure of your own inner guidance about the reality that would be in highest wisdom, simply request the natural highest Divine order to take place. Then let go and allow it to be. It is often referred to as 'Let Go and Let God'. This gives the right for your power and energy to be used for the purity of the highest Divine Light/ God/ All-that-Is.

As one gains in wisdom, one begins more and more to understand and accept authorship of the manifestations in one's world. As the truth of this becomes more a state of being, rather than something we have to keep reminding ourselves to apply in our lives, we will re-unite with the Creator Force of the Universe and take the final steps of learning in a third dimensional world. This leads to an ascension from this level of existence to the higher levels of beauty, peace and harmony.

When you deny that you create your own reality, you are denying a truth. Only the truth allows something to disappear. When we fail to take responsibility for our creations, we are adding a lie to the situation, which causes the thoughts and emotions concerned with it, to persist. The energy cannot dissipate, because it is not being viewed in its exact truth.

A common example may be seen in the traumatic break up of a relationship, where one partner appears to have been 'wronged'.

Let us say one of them has gone off with the best friend. This scenario is often full of judgements about the partner who left and the best friend, as well as denying even the remotest possibility that this situation could have been created by the person being 'abandoned'. This person is viewed as the poor victim who obviously had no control over the situation at all. This is not only a denial of the fact that we create and attract everything in our lives for our greater learning, but also in deciding that someone is a poor soul who has no control over his life, we deny their power and capability as a spiritual being. In this case, because the situation is not being viewed in truth, it cannot be resolved. We sometimes hear that an ex-partner 'remained hurt for many years', which shows us clearly that they continually failed to take responsibility for their creation. Perhaps we hear that they 'eventually got over it', which may mean they managed to bury it deep enough so it didn't hurt them anymore. When we deny responsibility for the things that occur in our world, we create solid, dense energies around us. This prevents us from experiencing much of the lightness, happiness, fun and joy that is a natural part of the Divine order of all life.

Perhaps you have a painful or sad situation in your life, in the past or present, that you have been saying was caused by someone other than yourself. To assess the truth of whether or not you 'create your own reality', why don't you begin right now to say to yourself, "I created that! I take full responsibility for attracting that into my life, in order that I learn to grow stronger and more loving". You may find it a bit difficult to begin with, as we sometimes have a tendency to make others wrong, wanting them to feel guilty and suffer for what they have 'done to us'. Don't put in any escape clauses that will help you blame 'him, her or them' in any way. **You did it**, regardless of the details – the entire overall episode was created by you and manifested into your world. If you wish, you could look and see what you learned or could still learn from that experience. **You will find that the goal of all learning is unconditional love.**

If you keep accepting the truth of your creation, the situation resolves itself. The energy will begin to dissipate and you will start to feel much better about it all. Fully accepting the fact that you created it will bring great realisations, excitement and joy.

Your acceptance and responsibility of the creation of everything in your life takes you into the Divine Universal Flow of complete happiness, abundance, joy and unconditional love for all Life. It will take you to a place of peace and contentment deep within. It takes you **Home.**

Now, as Earth proceeds into her new millennium of Peace and Harmony, it is time for everyone to begin to accept themselves as children of God and creators of reality, in order to co-create a world of Love.

CHAPTER SIX

The Masters and the Rays

M any legions of incarnate and discarnate Light beings serve this Universe. Although in truth there is no real 'location' for Spirit; the term is used to assist in bringing understanding. These beings who work in service to the Light are 'located' in all dimensions, assisting projects throughout the Universe.

The Great White Brotherhood consists of beings from various higher realms. Many of these beings, as well as other groups such as the Galactic Confederation, Space Brotherhood and other interplanetary missionaries and groups, assist the plan on Earth.

Many of the incarnated Light Force have begun to feel and remember the connections and agreements that have been made between the incarnated mission team and beings called Ascended Masters, Cosmic beings, Archangels, Lords and the Elohim. We have adopted the term 'Hierarchy' to signify these beings, whom we find 'located' from the 7th to the 12th dimensions Those we call the Ascended Masters are in the higher bands of the 7th dimension. They are considerable in number, but some have channelled a great deal of information since the 1930s and are therefore more familiar, such as St. Germain (Chohan of the 7th ray – the violet ray of freedom) and Kuthumi (a name from his incarnation as a Dutchman named as Koot Hoomi). Kuthumi was also St. Francis of Assisi and Pythagoras. He is the previous guardian of the yellow 3rd ray of wisdom and currently co-shares the role of World Teacher with Jesus, until the new millennium.

It is St. Germain who will oversee the next 2,000 year Aquarian Age on Earth. He assumes this responsibility fully at the end of the century, taking over this role from the being we know as Jesus Christ (his most famous incarnation), who has held this for the two thousand year Piscean Age.

Other better known Ascended Masters include El Morya, Hilarion, Jesus and his twin flame Lady Nada (she has not been incarnated here), Serapis Bey, Dwal Kuhl, Lady Portia (twin flame of St. Germain), Paul the Venetian and Mother Mary. Although naturally operating as androgynous energies, they communicate to us often as male and female identities, to assist reality on the lower levels. Cosmic beings from the 8th, 9th and higher dimensions such as Buddha, Pallas Athena, Lord Maitreya, Maha Chohan (he is also known as the Lord of Civilisation) Kwan Yin and Lao Tse, Helios and Vesta (the Sun), Melcezadek, Metranon and Sanat and Venus Kumara are part of the thousands assisting Earth at this time. One's own vibration rate determines the dimension one can reach.

A group called the Elohim are from very high levels and rarely communicate directly to Earth. Their guidance is passed down through various Cosmic beings. It is important to understand that lower dimensional beings can claim to be any of these masters (procedures for ascertaining correct identities are given in Chapter 10).

Many archangels are also involved, perhaps the more well known of these being Gabriel, Auriel, Raphael and the Lord Michael (Mikael) who represents the Divine Will of God, holding the sword of peace, protection and justice for Earth.

The Angelic Order begins with the **Seraphim,** angels from the very highest dimension who surround the throne of God. The **Cherubim** are the guardians and senders of divine Light from Heaven and the keepers of the celestial records. **Thrones** are the companion angels of the planets. **Dominions** serve to integrate the spiritual and material worlds and are the regulators of angelic duties. **Virtues** are the next angelic realm and are responsible for sending great amounts of divine energy where it is needed. **Powers** are the bearers of the conscience of humanity; these are the angels that assist with birth and death. **Principalities** are the guardian angels of large groups. They are integrators of a unified global order. **Archangels** are responsible for the overall pattern of human endeavour. **Angels** are the ones that most humans associate with as they are more closely connected with human affairs. These are our healers, guardians, protectors and friends, and each person on Earth has at least one angel responsible and caring for them.

Some lightworkers feel an affinity with specific realms or planets. The reason for this is that we all come from different areas and align with groups that are familiar to us. Some may find their interest focuses on the idea of ETs (extra-terrestrials). You may feel very strange on Earth and have a definite feeling that you do not belong here. This can indicate that you have come more recently from another planet or civilisation (sometimes an unusual and unheard of one) or you could be an 'ET walk-in'. This means a being who made an agreement prior to the incarnation, usually with a member of their own planet, that at a certain time they would 'walk in' to an existing adult body. The original occupant would return home. Often the incoming being is more evolved, has been working elsewhere and had no time (or desire) to proceed through the growth stages from babyhood. In this way they can comply with the Non-Intervention Law that one must be an inhabitant of a planet to be able to help change its evolution. Most are consciously aware they are a 'walk-in' and have fairly specific mission orders. Often they have an agreement to assist the awakening and cleansing of their own planetary extra terrestrial group, so that each of those can complete their own individual missions. These 'walk-ins' are all over the world and the majority are with the Light. They are quite often distinguishable, as many of them do not conform with or have an understanding of Earth patterns, feel quite alone and may behave in an outlandish way. Occasionally lightworkers attend a workshop designed for ETs, which can prove to be uncomfortable for the lightworker, as the ET reality, truth and manners sometimes conflict with 'accepted' Earth patterns. They feel no obligation to conform to your fixed realities. Not all ETs are 'walk-ins' and not all 'walk-ins' are ETs.

'Walk-ins' have always been a part of third dimensional existence. Under Universal law, it has always been possible for someone who expresses a wish to leave but does not wish to commit suicide, to be approached and asked if they truly desire this. They are asked over a period of time, more than once and usually in the sleep state which is the time of spiritual connection. If it is certain that this is required, the exchange takes place under very strict supervision of several guardians or custodians. A contract is drawn up that always requires the incoming being to complete the agreements and any unfinished tasks of the outgoing person. This does not apply to 'ET walk-ins' as the agreements are pre-arranged and different. Under normal procedures, the person will choose to take up the existing identity without retaining a conscious memory of the transaction. The incoming person picks up some of the patterns of the vacating person, thereby enabling him or her to carry on without too many obvious differences being observed in the personality. This isn't usually noticed by anyone, although it actually happens quite a lot. It is often passed off with expressions like 'he hasn't been himself lately'. If people don't expect these sort of things, they are often not seen.

Some lightworkers feel a closeness to the space fleet that patrol and assist this galaxy. In this case, it may be that they were a crew member prior to incarnating here. These spaceships are part of the Galactic Confederation and are generally commanded by beings from the fifth and the sixth dimensions. They are not Ascended Masters. The better known of these are Commanders Ashtar, Korton, Monka, Athena and Merku. Generally, these light ships are quite vast and different from the older style ships from smaller fleets, as normally depicted in our television shows. The mother ships are like small worlds. The large spaceship shown in the film "Close Encounters of the Third Kind" is closer to the true size.

You may be from the Angelic Kingdom. Although normally angels do not take human form, many have incarnated for this special planetary occasion. Some feel close to the angelic realms and the archangels and others may feel closer to the Ascended Masters. Some people feel a special connection to a **specific** Ascended Master or archangel, or perhaps feel they are this master or their twin flame. The reasons for this could be as follows:

1. Because you are following an evolutionary path that comes under the guidance and training of that being.
2. You may have incarnated using the specific energies of the particular ray for which that master is responsible.
3. This feeling of closeness could also be because you were incarnated during the same lifetime and worked together. Some of the masters spent many incarnations on this planet prior to their ascension.
4. You may have worked together before on other planetary missions. You may be a 'system buster' and have completed many planetary missions.
5. You may be an aspect of that master.

6. You may have a specific agreement with that being.
7. You are friends.
8. You feel a great love for this being.

The Rays

The rays are special energies available to serve this Universe. Each one has a specific range of vibration that shows itself in particular sounds and colours that parallel the rainbow. Each ray encompasses certain qualities and aspects of God. Until recently we have had seven rays available to us and seven of the Ascended Masters and Archangels are the guardians or chohans of these rays. A few years ago, some of the Ascended Masters who had held these rays for some time, began taking up new roles and some other masters replaced them. Now a further five rays are extended to Earth, to be incorporated for use in the new Age.

We incarnate using a specific ray and we reflect that particular aspect of God to other people. For most lightworkers the energies of these rays are also a personal evolutionary learning. If for example, you came in on the 5th ray of truth, you would find that you were quite a stickler for exact truth in your life, expecting it from yourself and others. As you combine more fully with your 'I Am' presence and incorporate the energies of this ray, you would find you require very precise truthful wording. This is because people on the truth ray understand the power of words and realise that only when something is precise can it be perfectly duplicated in time and space, which allows a cleansing to take place, dispersing unwanted energies and conditions. When the wording is even slightly off, pure truth is not present and the energy cannot dissipate. This is why, when we do not take responsibility for causing situations in our lives, we tend to hang on to the thoughts and energies until we view it in truth – as it really is. This is carried through different incarnations. When we blame someone else for something we created, as it is not the highest truth, it cannot be resolved. When we take responsibility and say 'I created that', from that moment it can begin to dissolve.

When we wish to work on a particular task, we tune into the specific energy that can assist us. For example, if you wished to work on opening the heart chakra, you could draw on the energy of the pink ray of Love.

The rays	Colour	Previous Cohan	Current Cohan
1 Will	Blue	El Morya	El Morya
2 Wisdom	Yellow	Kuthumi	Lord Lanto
3 Love	Pink	Lady Nada	Paul the Venetian
4 Purity	White	Serapis Bey	Serapis Bey
5 Truth	Green	Hilarion	Hilarion
6 Devotion	Red	Jesus	Lady Nada
7 Freedom	Violet	St. Germain	St. Germain

Every missionaire has come in on at least one of these rays. This means that he or she holds that aspect of God deep within their heart and will have purposes and goals concerning that quality, as well as carry that energy within their auric field. You will reflect in your words and actions the particular quality of God that the ray encompasses. You can carry all seven, but this would be very exceptional. By studying the various qualities of the rays you can see which are prominent in your life.

There are five new rays penetrating the Earth, each with its own unique qualities. People are now beginning to adopt some of these incoming qualities. The new rays are to be mainly utilised to assist this planet into her new dimension and will be used by those who will carry on their evolution in the fifth dimension. Some people, whilst in their sleep state, are perceiving these new colours coming to Earth. It can be a little frustrating when we find that these magnificently alive colours seen during sleep cannot be seen or re-created during their daytime experience.

The Five New rays	Colour
8 Clarity	Aquamarine
9 Harmony and Balance	Magenta
10 Eternal Peace	Gold
11 Divine Purpose and Joy	Peach
12 Transformation	Opalescence

The masters that preside over the guardians of the 12 rays are the Maha Cohan, Maitreya and Buddha in ascending order. Above these, we find Sanat Kumara, the Ancient of Days and Planetary Logos of Earth. Sanat Kumara connects Heaven (Shamballa) and

Earth by reflecting the state of awareness of humanity to the spiritual mind of God.

The Energy Shifts

There are vast energies reaching the Earth at this time to assist the transition. There have also been many special dispensations of energy granted by the Hierarchy that oversees this operation; to assist with cleansing and balancing of both the Earth and individuals. These energy shifts are often presented to the conscious awareness of the Light Force or carried through messengers who have agreed to this task. Often a particular day or a short period of time is chosen to focus or meditate upon. By joining together, sometimes physically and sometimes in a spiritual connection and concentrating on a particular focus, we greatly assist the entire project.

The new age began its real shift in the 1960s, as people began to reach for a new awareness. In their search for peace and love, a tremendous shift in consciousness occurred that resulted in the growth of the hippie movement, flower power and psychedelic drugs. This represented a major breakaway from past traditions.

In 1987 a messenger in South America called Jose Arguelles, presented to the world a special energy day called the Harmonic Covergence. Many hundreds of thousands gathered throughout the world to focus on peace and a great shift in consciousness occurred.

Another important energy shift occurred on the 11th January 1992. In 1991, a messenger named Solara from the U.S.A did an excellent job travelling around the world awakening lightworkers. She told the Light Force that they needed to come together on the 11th January at 11am and 11pm, to perform specific actions in order to open a major dimensional doorway. On this day called 11:11, set long ago, a certain critical mass number of lightworkers (spokespeople for the planet) were required to say a 'Yes' for this planet, as part of its movement toward ascension. Although people were called to its key focus points in Egypt and New Zealand, it also asked for many other groups to link in throughout the world. It is estimated that about 4,500 groups came together on that day and the doorway was opened.

Many of those who participated had the number 11:11 pre-encoded in their etheric blueprint a long time ago. This helped trigger the memory that they were meant to help. Many lightworkers had this number continually presented to them in various ways, such as every time they looked at a digital clock it happened to show 11:11. It is interesting to see that 11:11 is inscribed either side of the doorway of the ancient pyramid in Egypt where the key activation point was required to be held. If any lightworker meant to help was still asleep on that date, or had not picked up on the signs, another stepped in to take their place. Some people were 'drafted' into the role even minutes before 11am on the 11th, in order that the required numbers were met. This focus continues as further doorways are opened and many still see 11:11 signs in their life.

Many other dispensations of energy occurred between 1992 and 1994. During 1993 there were four principal ones, of love, power, wisdom and freedom, one for each quarter of the year.

Another shift of energy occurred when one million lightworkers gathered in fifty-eight countries across the world to chant the sacred universal sound of the OM (Aum) for 8 minutes at 12 Noon GMT on the 21st August, 1994. The date chosen by the ascended realms for this event was the 2,000th birthday of Jesus Christ, who was actually born on the 21st August 7 BC. Thousands gathered at the main focus point of this energy in Wembley Arena in London, UK. The sounding of the OM was led by eighty sisters and brothers of the Brahma Kumaris World Spiritual University, dressed in white. 'The OM' is known as the voice of God and is said to be the sound that holds the entire Universe in balance. It is the Hindu symbol for God and is held as sacred in many religions, including Buddhism. The plan was to create a vortex of a depth necessary to reach down into the energy grid of the Earth. Wembley was chosen because a partial vortex already existed there, created by various previous lightworker concerts and gatherings. The energy lines were being used to transmit the sound of the OM across the Earth. Its purpose was to help bring any discordant energies back into harmony and balance. This world-wide event included linking groups at many strategic locations around the world, to ensure that the sound was carried from the vortex at Wembley out to the extremities of the Earth. An incredible event took place as the Mother Earth took control of the energies across the world and kept the OM going for 15 minutes. This also occurred in many other locations all over the world. The result of people continuing to do the OM for this extra time, was that the OM itself increased in frequency and the entire Earth moved to a new space and a higher frequency. This also took a further 45 minutes off each day. You may feel that we have reached into the higher frequency of the HU, known as the universal sound for the 'in breath' (moving back toward God).

The event at Wembley changed the lives of people present who experienced the love, joy, unity and healing throughout the 8 hour concert, the meditation and the unbelievably powerful OM. On the 24th August, 3 days later, peace came to Ireland as the IRA announced an end to violence, perhaps assisted by this day and its link-in events in Dublin and other parts of Ireland. Although we have since seen hiccups in this and some other peace processes in the world, understand that these things always have a higher picture. It is necessary for the **people** of these areas to demand peace.

There are many dates and times being set aside to help focus on peace for the world. Different groups and individuals receive various inspirations in communicating these energies to the rest of the Light Force. We have a Peace Clock, a Minute for Peace, Peace the 21st, the Silent Minute, Love for all the World on St. Valentines Day, a Moment for Prayer, the Wesak Festival, Full Moon meditation, and many other wonderful initiatives handling specific areas, such as the excellent issues by Da Vid of The Global Peace Foundation in California and the Marine Meditation begun by David Adams in Australia. This Marine Meditation focus, originated by the Ascended Master St. Germain in 1992, asks everyone around the world to meet at 8pm local time on the March and September Equinox every year to focus light into all the oceans and seas of the world. This timing effectively forms a twenty-four hour wave of oneness, healing and love that encircles the whole planet.

The energy now available is tremendous and is reaching this planet at approximately 11 waves per second. One can relate this in terms of power to an ocean wave which hits the shore at 1 wave every 30 seconds. The maximum energy level will be 14 waves per second at the height of the dimensional shift.

The cleansing and power of Light on Earth has **negated** the possibilities of nuclear war, great flooding of land masses, earthquake devastation or an axis tilt causing a pole shift.

This has been achieved through the extensive work done by the incarnated Light Force in the form of gatherings, large and small; to meditate and focus Light; the energy work done at many Earth locations; with great use of sound, colour and crystals; the use of the transmuting violet flame; positive thoughts and the healing benefits coming from all the mission tasks. Accompanied by the Divine dispensations of energy and the help given by the angels and ascended realms of Light, a great cleansing has taken place.

Solely due to the mediations by the incarnated Light Force, there is a great wall of Light extending out around the Earth for 107.4 miles (November, 1996). This prevents any negative Earth energy going out into the galaxy, but allows higher frequency light to enter. The denser energies contained within the Earth are being totally transmuted within her structure and the Earth now emanates a lovely violet hue.

It was the Earth Mother herself (the being whose body is the whole of Earth) who originated the request for assistance. Long ago she called to the highest on High for help to cleanse the negative energy imbalance from Earth to allow her and all her life forms to continue their evolution and ascend into the higher frequency of the 5th dimension.

Her original options to cleanse the negative energies were:

1. To choose to accept light, love, harmony, balance, peace, prayer and healing from all the many sources offering it. This choice allows the Earth to use Light to transmute the negative energies, thereby allowing a very peaceful and gentle cleansing.
2. To choose great flooding, fires, earthquakes and possibly requiring the tilt of the Earth's axis, which would re-locate the North and South Poles, causing massive devastation. This choice would involve great pain and suffering for the Earth herself, humanity and the billions of life forms connected to the Earth.

As one would expect, the Earth Being has chosen to make the transition into her new dimension in the gentlest manner possible, through the use of Light. She gratefully acknowledges and accepts with immense love all the work done on Earth to help her. She is very happy to continue with this option, receiving as much help as each is willing to give. It doesn't take a great deal of wisdom to know what form of cleansing she or anyone else would choose. It is not pleasant to hear the cries of pain and suffering of humans and all the flora and fauna being ripped apart in traumatic geophysical upheavals. The level of gentleness with which she proceeds is dependent on the amount of Light received.

The Earth chooses to birth gently into her new dimension. The Light Force on Earth, representing the soul families on Earth, by following Spirit are able to decide what is best in the Divine Order. With continued positive creation by the Light Force, God prevails.

CHAPTER SEVEN

The Path of Initiation and Testing

All starseeds and lightworkers follow a Path of Initiation towards ascension. It is up to each individual to grasp the opportunity being presented and understand the concept being shown, to learn the lesson and move on. The various stages take different time periods to transcend, depending on the ability of the person to master the lessons.

Many are aware that Jesus incarnated to introduce the Age of Pisces. This was a time for people to become aware of the concept of 'love thy brother as thyself'. This was a movement to bring a deeper compassion and understanding throughout mankind. There were also other reasons not so well known. Because it was known that when he combined with his 'I Am' presence around his 30th year, his vibrational capacity would be extremely high, the plan was for him to then carry a high vibrational blueprint that would raise the ceiling of Light on Earth. You could say that, previously to this, the human population was crushed by the heavy density (caused by negativity) around them. This would make it easier for the population to move upwards into a new higher frequency.

By the pattern of his life, he also symbolically showed each step we have to take on the path to ascension. Everyone follows these steps in his/her own awakening process. There is no specific length of time it takes to complete each step, because everyone chooses their own pace.

The stages of this process are as follows:

The Birth of Christ
This relates to the birth of the Christ within. It is that first moment of realising that you are something more than you had previously

thought. This symbolises the recognition of the Three-Fold Flame deep within the heart. The Three-Fold Flame represents the blue ray of the power and Divine Will of God, the yellow ray of wisdom and the pink ray of love. This flame is our connection to the Divine Source.

The Baptism

This is the first conscious decision we make to purify the physical, emotional, mental and spiritual bodies. It could be a decision to begin eating healthier food, to take a flower essence to help cleanse our emotions and mental patterns, or read a book on positive thinking. This begins a change in our vibrational pattern, opening up a new awareness that allows more Light into our life.

Transfiguration

This is the commitment one makes to begin the search for truth. Some start on this step and move continuously forward, while others may choose gaps of several years throughout this stage. Whatever the circumstances, this stage is rarely abandoned permanently. Once this process is started it can become almost obsessive. This is the stage where lots of books are read, many courses are attended and one can get involved in philosophies, cults or mainstream religion in a search for answers.

It is also the beginning of 'three stages of testing' that take place on this route to ascension. This first stage challenges your commitment and the sincerity of your decision to come to Earth as a lightworker. Can you be relied upon to carry out your tasks and agreements, even if difficulties arise?

Imagine a situation of being in the front line during a war, when you would really need the assurance that your team members would not desert you. You may be on a particular manoeuvre when you were relying on them to provide cover for you, but because of some particularly heavy opposition, they fled. In a way the situation is similar. You need to be able to be counted on and not weaken in the face of adversity. There is a saying 'When the going gets tough, the tough get going'. This is the easiest stage of the testing path.

The Garden

This was the time Jesus went alone for forty days into the garden to meditate and be still, to gain wisdom and greater connection to the Divine Source. This is the time in your life when you must stand alone. Family and friends will desert you and you will have no-one to help you face your situations or give you assistance in your decision making. You will receive no help from any source other than your own spiritual connection to the Divine Source. This means neither human nor angel will assist. All have agreed that for your greater good they will not assist at this time. This can be a time of working through great problems and sorrows, always with the option of moving into stillness to seek the answers and the wisdom within.

Your faith, love and trust are greatly tested in two ways. The first is your ability to maintain a spiritual viewpoint of unconditional love toward any friends, family and beings in the ascended realms who appear to have deserted you and let you down. The second is in your trust of the divine perfection of all things, in your knowing that everything that happens in your life is perfect and for your highest good.

This level is the most difficult stage of the testing. The degree of testing can vary enormously because various factors come into play at this point. One factor is how much cleansing has already been done up to this point. If there is still a great deal to clear, this stage can seem very tough because the emotional and mental bodies are getting stripped away at the same time. It may also be that you have chosen some pretty tough tasks and you need to be toughened in preparation for them. You can either have a very easy time of it or you may feel you are being pushed past the limits of endurance. It is possible to have experiences that cannot be explained either to yourself or others. You may also feel that you are going through a very traumatic negative experience and 'you' seem to be lost in there somewhere. This is how it can seem, without the understanding that comes later.

The answer is simple. Can you maintain a spiritual viewpoint whilst under pressure? Can you remain in service to God under pressure? Can you be unconditionally loving, no matter the circumstances?

If you continue to hold the focus of Light and not give in to the temptation to let it go in order to get some peace; if you can hold your spiritual viewpoint and be aware you are invincible; you will not only endure it, but will come to a great place of peace and joy. You will also become 'yourself' again and will in the end, believe it or not, realise that the experience was positive and has helped you enormously.

The Crucifixion

This time involves a letting go of the burdens of the world. Many lightworkers feel that if they don't keep struggling on, the whole plan will fall apart. It is easy to get the feeling that you are the only one available to get the job done and this thought often weighs heavily on the shoulders.

When operating in the Divine Flow, doing only what excites, interests or feels right, you discover your role here is not a burden to be borne, but a sheer joy. If you are feeling the 'weight of responsibility', you could well be in this part of the initiation process. If you are thinking you 'should' or 'must' do something, you are in a thought process that you have mistaken for responsibility. This is not the true responsibility which comes naturally with evolution and carries with it feelings of ease, confidence and lightness. It requires no 'thought' process and is simply what one naturally does in life.

This stage of initiation requires you to recognise areas where you may have accepted responsibility that really belongs to others and that you hand it back to them. It is time for each individual to take back their power. If you go on carrying responsibilities for others, you are **not really helping them.** You are, in a sense, saying that they are too weak to do it themselves and you are preventing their opportunity to become stronger. Additionally, you may be blocking their ascension path and preventing them from handling the karma necessary to bring their energies back into balance. When you decided to accept their responsibility as your own, you also adopted the relevant karma. Even if you have accepted the karmic absolution that has been granted to the majority of the Light Force, this would not extend to cover karma that truly belonged to another. If you continued to take on this responsibility you could accrue further karma, by impeding their evolutionary progress.

You need to recognise and accept your own responsibilities. These show themselves by a feeling of excitement, rightness and interest in their contemplation. Responsibilities you have that truly belong to others show up when they feel like burdens to you and require lots of effort and overcoming of difficulties to get them done. The contemplation of these tasks is more likely to bring a sigh of resignation than a feeling of excitement.

If one listens to the dictates of the mind, it is easy to get the idea that there is 'no-one else that can do it'. So one falls into the trap of taking on other people's tasks and in doing so, moves out of the flow of Divine spiritual guidance. If it is truly your task, it feels right and is accomplished with ease. If you are operating as spirit and without ego you will work in pure inspiring joy. This is the final part of the testing.

The Resurrection

It is at this point that, whilst still in the physical body, one makes a greater connection with the **'Christ – I Am Presence'**. The lower subtle bodies are in the latter stages of purification and the goals of the higher Self are taking precedence over desires of the incarnated soul identity. To the extent that this has occurred and the 'I Am' presence with its integrity and alignment to the Source is in control, is to the degree that the gifts of mastery and grace are given. All the abilities that you need to complete the tasks on Earth will be given to you. All the programmes that you laid in for this plan will now be accessible. It doesn't matter whether you need to have knowledge of herbs, crystals, powerful energy sites, essences, an understanding of higher mathematics, or just to be still and balanced; you will have what you require in each moment to carry out your task. If you do not appear to have the abilities you need, check that you are still operating as Spirit and haven't gone back into the ego or the 'think' process.

The Ascension

You will ascend when:

1. You have completed your Earth Mission.
2. The lower bodies are purified. This means that all of these bodies now contain enough Light to raise yourself into a higher existence. The specifics of this purification depends on whether you have chosen the old or new method of ascension. For those choosing to ascend without the physical body, only the three lower bodies (emotional, mental and lower spiritual) need to be in the level of Light referred to. For those who have chosen to transmute the **physical** body, then this would also need purifying.
3. Your intention is pure.
4. Karma is balanced and complete at 51% or acceptance of karmic absolution (if applicable).

The karmic requirement for planet Earth has been altered. It has been difficult for the population of Earth to achieve a karmic balance of energies, owing to the negative energy imbalance of this planet. The Ascended Master St. Germain, part of the spiritual hierarchy of Earth, approached a Light council known as the Karmic Board and asked as an act of Grace, for the population of Earth to have the karmic requirement for completion reduced from 100% to 51%. After some deliberation and attempts and consequent failures by members of the Karmic Board to spend some time on Earth and try to leave with a clear karma, this was duly granted.

Recently, in addition to this, as an act of Divine dispensation, **karmic absolution has been offered to the Light Force on Earth.**

Universal Law states that free will and choice are never violated. This means that you would need to **accept** this offer of karmic absolution before it can manifest in your life. It is a choice.

Karmic absolution is granted to all. However, the first point of choice is with your 'I Am' presence. This is the part of you that is not incarnated and can always see the higher picture of what is best for the incarnated soul. Whilst 97.8% of the entire Light Force now have this option, there are a few instances where the 'I Am' presence of some individuals felt it would be more beneficial for their growth and highest learning to experience the energies involved in their **last remaining few percent** of karma. Make no judgements about this. It is not a punishment, but is truly a gift. For those few individuals, understand that your 'I Am' presence knows you and what you truly want. There may be many different reasons. Some have come later to the planet and wish to experience as much learning as they can fit in. Others were adamant prior to incarnating, about specific lessons they wished to learn. Just trust that all is in perfect order and that whatever is for you, is for your highest good. As some people still have belief patterns that tell them they are unworthy, it may not be easy to know if you have this option or not. Therefore, it is suggested that you proceed **as though you have this option.** If it is meant to occur, it will.

The steps to take to accept Karmic Absolution.

1. Be still in meditation. Focus on the etheric flame within your heart that connects you to the Source. Flood this flame with the vibration of Love.
   Say aloud with power: – **"I invoke my mighty 'I Am' presence. By the grace of God I accept the Divine dispensation of karmic absolution."**

2. When you entered this incarnation, the Veils of Maya (forgetting) were still present. At that time, you were still unawakened as to your true role here. This is because generally speaking, the original agreement for you to awaken to the specific truth that you are here on a mission, was to be in the last decade of the current millennium. You also didn't know that karmic absolution was to be offered to the Light Force.
   Naturally therefore, you set into play all the energies necessary to achieve karmic balance, prior to completing your mission role here. This meant you made agreements with others to interact with you, to bring about this balance. Many of these agreements have finished, some are currently in progress and others are winging their way toward you. Therefore it is further suggested that as a second step, you ask your 'I Am' presence – **"I invoke my mighty 'I Am' presence and where it be in highest Divine order, I ask that all beings that still have agreements with me regarding the balancing of my karma, are contacted now to**

be asked if they are willing to release these agreements." Asking for highest order will then keep intact any agreements that will be beneficial. They have free will and choice to accept or not. However, as they will be approached on a higher level and will understand the reason for the request, it is likely that they will accept.

You are **not** now exempt from karma. One has a responsibility to maintain integrity within the Divine Flow to ensure that no further imbalance occurs. Further positive and negative karma can still be accrued, but you will find it is being quickly balanced – as 'instant karma'. We tend to forget that karma can also be 'good' and we can accrue lots of 'brownie points' and spent magical lifetimes with lots of wonderful things happening.

At the moment of ascension, one is left alone to make the final decision to ascend. The feeling is of being completely alone. It was at this point of ascension where Jesus, suddenly feeling the abandonment of all presences, called out from the cross "Father, why hast thou forsaken me?" As the choice is made, one begins to ascend.

At this point you will re-unite with your twin flame and the two of you will walk together through the Flames of Ascension ceremony and the state of ascension into the fifth dimension is fully attained.

The twin flames who have completed all the learning **that can only be obtained by being separated from each other,** are now destined to remain together. Now they may resume the evolutionary position they had reached prior to beginning this Earth mission, or through greater wisdom and learning they may have attained a new level.

Those who have not completed this learning will still re-unite with the twin at this stage. However, at some point they will probably choose to complete this learning, which would mean a further period of separation from the twin. (also covered in Chapter 11)

Upon completion of their individual mission tasks, the Light Force upon Earth will re-unite with their twin flames. You may now choose to be anywhere, doing anything you wish, for as long as you like.

It is time to go home.

CHAPTER EIGHT

Discernment and the Power Within
'Discernment' – *the key word on the planet*

Using the Power Within

To establish the power within, lightworkers only need to follow their own inner guidance, intuition, feeling of rightness, excitement, spirit or heart – 100% of the time, without reservation – in total faith and trust.

The greatest gift of pure Spirit is the love, power and wisdom of the Source. This magnificent Three-Fold Flame lies within us all. It is our connection to the Source/ All-That-Is/ God or whatever you choose to call Divine creation. This is the source of our accurate intuitive knowing, available to each of us in every moment.

It is always present and it is we who choose:
a) Whether we are balanced enough to perceive it and
b) Whether we wish to follow the Divine Flow or our own will (Thy Will or my will).

The need to be discerning and accept only what feels right, is necessary for your own personal evolutionary progress, your agreements with others and your purpose here on Earth.

1. **Keep a positive perspective.** There are millions of loving, exquisite, special lightworkers all over the Earth. They are awakened and lovingly dedicated to their service on Earth. The vast majority of the entire Earth's population want to live in peace and harmony.
2. **Everyone in the universe is equal** – this includes you.
3. **Be a master.** Follow your intuition.
4. **Realise that you always know** when the energy being offered is loving and feels right. It is instinctive and usually immediate.
5. **Realise that you always know** when someone or something is offering an energy that you would prefer not to support. This is

also instinctive and usually immediate. Often the 'think' process comes in at this point, and we try to find a logical reason why we must have got it wrong. Sometimes we dismiss it by telling ourselves we are not being very loving or trusting. Sometimes we lack the confidence to trust our own perception, especially if everyone around us is of a different opinion. You will be a master when you trust your own intuition and will stand by it, even if everyone else in the whole world says it is not so. There are millions of people around the world holding the same inaccurate belief patterns, so popularity doesn't necessarily signify pure truth.

6. **Neutral vibration.** Realise that if you cannot feel a 'good' or 'bad' vibration, you may be experiencing a **neutral** vibration. Your next question could be **why?** Is this neutral vibration covering up an energy that is trying to remain concealed? Is the energy behind it, positive or negative?

7. **Discernment is not judgement.** The aim is intuitively to perceive the energy being presented and decide whether you choose to support it or not. For the highest good, you need to decide whether to add your energy and power to that person, project, workshop, tape, article, lecture, conversation, group, belief system, government, etc. If there is the slightest doubt about it, it is better to wait until you are certain, rather than jumping in and having to extricate yourself later. To observe that something is an energy that you choose not to work with, does not require that you make a judgement that it is 'bad'. You could view it simply as an alternative energy available to experience in this Universe, one that you do not wish to work with. In choosing to withdraw your energy, power and support from a particular area, doesn't mean you also need to withdraw your unconditional love.

8. **Don't be impressed,** thereby falling into the pattern of thinking that others know more than you. Regardless of who they are/ how famous/ how many books they have written/ how many workshops they've held/ whomever they are channelling or think they are channelling/ how powerful, intelligent, plausible or intellectual it sounds – **does it feel right?** You have a 100% ability to ascertain whether something resonates as true or not for you. There are wonderful lecturers and authors delivering

exquisite concepts of truth, but it will always be you who must choose whose reality to align with.

There are two energies currently operating within the 3rd dimensional reality (the 3rd is the solid world we see around us).

One energy chooses love, peace and harmony, reaching toward truth and a greater connection to the Source and the Light. This energy chooses to blend ego with Spirit, toward a greater service to others.

The other chooses a pattern of limitation that requires keeping 'control of' and 'power over', generally through the use of fear, through misinformation, keeping people in ignorance of their true nature as spiritual beings. Their objective is to distance you from the Source and the Light.

Simply perceive the type of energy and act intuitively, in the Divine Flow. **There can never be an excuse good enough to withdraw unconditional love,** no matter what anyone is saying or doing. If you do make a judgement and remain unloving, you will at some point, have to attract the same lesson into your life until you can love *unconditionally.*

If our life runs along positive thinking patterns, we will usually only experience loving energies around us. If we still have any negative patterns present, there is a possibility we will come across this second type of energy.

It serves no purpose to deny the existence of the second type of energy or the fact that some people prefer to work with this energy. At this time on Earth, it would be naive not to perceive this energy where it exists. This is a failure to use discernment and confusion will ensue. **However,** there is no reason to give this area credibility and power that it does not have. The further one moves away from the Source, the heavier one's density becomes and therefore the ability to experience real love and true power. These levels usually experience **conditional** love and **power over,** obtained through the use of fear. They have no real power compared to Light, but only what they can make others believe they have. Just as when a light is switched on in a room and the darkness is no more, so in the presence of Light, denser energies dissolve into the higher light frequency.

The higher your evolution, the more you will experience greater Light and connection to the Source/All-That-Is and to the availability of Universal Power, bringing wisdom and the ease of responsibility. Incidentally, responsibility is joyful when it comes naturally with evolution, rather than through the mind insisting you 'should be' or 'must be' responsible.

Many of those currently incarnated on Earth were also here in the time of Atlantis. Halloween is actually All Hallows' Eve, the 31st October, the night before the continent of Atlantis sank. This is why Halloween is represented by ghosts and witches.

These old Atlanteans (great ocean lovers) are making sure that discernment and wisdom are used now on Earth, to take full advantage of this wonderful opportunity now to take this planet into full Light. They may even seem a little suspicious and untrusting at times as they check and double check. These ones are trying to make sure that what happened in Atlantis, through naiveté and a failure to discern differing energies, does not occur again.

You will always need to discern the energies that enter your world. It is up to you to act as a master and not need help every step of the way. Once you are following your inner guidance, it comes naturally and requires no effort whatsoever.

If everyone practised discernment, acting on their own authority, simply accepting whatever resonated as true and discarding the rest, everyone would move more quickly to a state of peace. Negative energies would have no platform from which to disseminate their misinformation.

Someone who lives without any confusion around them, being discerning without judging, loving all life and living in their creation of positive energy, will have inner tranquillity, peace and joy. This inner peace and light is seen by all.

Senior to the discussion regarding negative energy, is the higher truth that we create reality in the 'now'.

Your words and actions, when in highest truth and without confusion, will take the Divine Plan on Earth to the most wondrous state of glory ever witnessed in the Universe.

CHAPTER NINE

The Right to Decree and Universal Law

The Right to Decree is a right held by all those who work in service to the Light. It is part of the original agreement made by the planetary team that are here to assist the birth of this planet into her new dimensions.

The use of this right gives the ascended realms the power to move from the confines of the Law of Non-Intervention and act on our behalf. Only the inhabitants of a planet have the right to decide what may or may not occur for that planetary system.

It is a fast, powerful way to gain assistance from the great force of Light in the higher dimensions.

For it to work, it needs to be said three times (the power of three) and needs to be worded so that it is placed within universal law. It also needs to be aligned with the power of the Divine Light. It is wise to also bring it within the Law of Grace, just in case what you ask for is not for the highest good. You may not be able to see the higher picture and inadvertently ask for something that is not optimum for all concerned. The Law of Grace is opposite to the Law of Karma. If you ask for something to be placed under the Law of Grace you are asking for the setting aside, of any possible karmic repercussions this act may have upon yourself.

Examples:

"By Divine decree, in the name of God, under the Law of Grace, I ask for ...."(three times) "So be it. It is done."

"By Divine decree, in the name of the Holy Christ Light and under the Law of Grace, I ask the Ascended realms of Light to assist with ....". (three times) "So be it. It is done."

"By Divine decree, in the name of the Divine Mother/ Father God, under the Law of Grace, I ask the Angelic Kingdom .....Ascended Masters ...St. Germain ...Jesus ...Archangel Michael .....Kuthumi

.....Mother Mary .....my 'I Am' presence ....." (or whoever you please) (three times) "It is done."

You may ask for anything, for anyone, any country, any situation, anywhere.

If you ask for it from a place of love and it is highest wisdom for the ascended realms to act, it will be done. As the higher realms can always see the higher picture, they will choose the optimum way to help. It will therefore not always be the way you may assume is best. It is a good idea not to make expectations as to the outcome, or you may experience a loss or feel that the decree did not work, when it doesn't turn out as you thought it 'should'.

You don't need to 'think' about it after you have decreed. Don't tie up your energy by following it along. Simply intuitively decree as it feels right to do so and then having handed it over to the higher realms, let it go. Let go and let God. When you hand something over to God, it is not then necessary to keep checking up to see if God is handling it satisfactorily. In this way, you can be fully present in the 'now', ready to perceive the next right thing for you to say or do.

It is in the greatest wisdom to follow universal law at all times. This is the Divine Flow that always follows the greatest good.

Some other Universal laws are: the Law of Vibration, Attraction, (everything you put out, follows a curve like a boomerang and comes back to you), Abundance, Free Will and Choice, Group Endeavour, Manifestation, Ascension, Unity, Goodwill, Right Human Relations, Spiritual Approach, Essential Divinity, As Above – So Below; Rights: (many rights including The Right to one's Own Space, The Right to Challenge, etc.); The Law of Balance, Grace (waives the Law of Karma), Identity, Cause and Effect (Karma), Divine Love and Oneness.

Moving in the Divine flow is a moment by moment following of Spirit, saying and doing only that which comes from the heart and brings a feeling of rightness, interest or enthusiasm. Let go of the seriousness and have lots of fun. It is truly time to step onto the ray of joy and love.

CHAPTER TEN

Channelling, Protection and the Universal Challenge

There were agreements made long ago that certain material would be channelled from the ascended realms of Light, to trigger an awakening in the starseeds and lightworkers on Earth. The Ascended Masters promised they would reach us using various forms of energy, including channelling. Much of this work began in the 1930s, and has continued to this day. The books *A Course in Miracles* and then the *'I AM'* series (the green books) contain all the necessary truth for anyone to ascend from Earth. Although many people had earlier spiritual awakenings, the main time of awakening to the realisation that you are part of a great team of Light here to help Earth, began as recently as 1990. There was a major triggering in October of that year. It has continued intently since that time and now the majority of the Light Force on Earth are awakened.

A great deal of cleansing of the fixed patterns and rigid beliefs that lightworkers have adopted since incarnating here has taken place over these last few years. Many lightworkers have reached the stage where they are now taking up all their tasks and agreements. This may be just one or a series of quite different tasks. The main focus of most tasks now moves from inner cleansing of self, to concentrating on assisting those of humanity who need to gain a new spiritual awareness and reconnection to God.

Some lightworkers' tasks involve agreements made long ago to act as channels or receivers for this awakening material. In addition to those with original agreements, others are now bringing through this information.

Naturally, because of Earth's conditions of duality, whilst there is a great deal of beautiful and loving channelled material, there is also misinformation being channelled. If you concede that there are two energies at work, then you realise that two energies would

100

be channelling information. Sometimes negative energy is not obvious or clearly visible. Your lesson in wisdom is the discernment between these different energies.

It is the evolutionary level of the source of the information that reflects the level and purity of the truth being relayed. The higher the evolution, the wider the overall picture that is seen and the purer the truth.

There are thirteen dimensions in this Universe (the 13th being in a state of formation) and many levels within each dimension. To grasp this concept, one could visualise the Universe as a large square with denser, slower moving energy at the base, gradually getting finer as you proceed upwards to pure Light at the top. You could imagine beings located in any position within this square. The lower bands would represent the third and fourth dimension (which contains the astral plane) and the top bands would be the twelfth and the new thirteenth dimension. As you would imagine, it is more difficult to 'see' through heavy, dense energy. The lighter and finer the energy, the easier and further one could 'see'. As you become wiser and move into finer levels of light, your vibration allows you to see into higher dimensions. In truth, all dimensions exist in the same space, simultaneously.

A lot of channelled information is received from beings in the astral plane and fourth dimension. The Ascended Masters and Cosmic beings of Light we normally reach, are 'located' in the 7th, 8th and 9th dimensional planes. For greater ease of communication, the Ascended realms may use the fifth dimension as a bridging position between themselves and the third dimension. They would however when challenged, state their position or level as being the dimension they are truly from (which would be the 7th, 8th or 9th). It is therefore always advisable to establish the level of the being from whom one is receiving a communication.

Channelled material can also be greatly altered as it passes through the belief patterns, considerations, opinions and ideas of the person 'receiving' the material. If the 'channel' can really let go and just allow the communication to come through, a fair degree of purity is possible. In the majority of cases, the person acting as a channel would be unaware that they have filtered it through their own patterns and may have altered it. Most would deny emphatically that it is anything other than exactly as delivered. It is certainly not their conscious intention to change it. It can occur in such a subtle way that is not perceived by the 'channel'.

It is possible to check your own channelling by asking for the percentage of accuracy you are delivering. To get an accurate answer you would first need to release any 'fixed belief' you may have that you are delivering a perfect duplication. Also be willing to release any need to have a reply that it is being perfectly received. Honesty with yourself is required. If you did establish that some alteration was taking place, you would be able to fix it by letting go a little more to the Divine will. This would then establish a clearer line to the Source, helping yourself and anyone else to whom you were passing the information.

Under universal law, it is not permitted for Spirit to channel material that would force a change in the evolution of the person acting as the 'channel'. All content is confined to the current capacity of the mind of that person, including their education and vocabulary.

A partial exception to this occurs when the person receiving is willing to act as a 'trance channel'. In this case the 'receiver' leaves their body for the period of the transmission of the communication and the being originating the material, enters it. The being who has vacated has therefore no conscious knowledge of the information that has been imparted and so is not affected by its content. In order to know what they said during this time, these people would need to have the session taped and then listen to it later. This then places them in the same position as anyone else hearing the material. There are several well known 'trance channels', such as Daryl Anka channelling 'Bashar' and Jack Purcell channelling 'Lazaris'. Because the material is not being filtered through a maze of belief patterns, it can come through 'as delivered'. The trance channel's voice tends to be unusual, because the incoming being has to bring through data translated into the language needed and has to use the voice of the body being used. As one gets used to this 'accent' it can become quite endearing and it is nice to get an unfiltered truth. The level of truth from some trance channels is a joy to behold. Of course, negative energy forces can use any form of channelling, 'trance' included.

All channelling comes under the rule of universal law and this includes a great protection of the body and mind of the 'trance channel'. The Ascended Masters tend not to use trance channelling as a method. They seem to prefer a more conscious participation, perhaps because as we approach the last phase of this programme here on Earth, there is more of an accent on taking responsibility for the material channelled and becoming a master in one's own right. This is not to imply that 'trance channels' are not becoming masters, but that they have made different agreements. Some people channel communications that are delivered through the 'heart' that may or may not contain words. In these cases a flow of energy is passed from the ascended being through the channel. Some who prefer to operate more through the mind, are given the information with a more logical understanding. Some channels use both. Both are independently useful, as some people respond to a flow of love and others prefer to understand through a logical approach. A person who has a good grasp of science could bring through very detailed technical information. Both the words and the feelings can heal. Sometimes people listening later to a channelled session on audio tape can experience the healing energy.

Some people respond to a soft, gentle voice and others to a more authoritative, powerful voice and this is taken into account when bringing through material. Similar material is therefore sometimes given several times, using different channels and also different Ascended Masters as the different energies and voices reach different people. All this trouble is taken to ensure that everyone is reached. The higher beings are aware that our belief patterns can get in the way of receiving material. For example, perhaps you've heard someone say they just couldn't listen to a tape because they didn't like the accent. Perhaps you have heard, "It couldn't be so and so channelling because it doesn't sound gentle enough", "Because they wouldn't have that sort of humour" or even perhaps, "They don't have a sense of humour" (why ever not?)

Although not many channels bring through the information exactly as it was received, the percentage is 'weighed up' from the higher levels. It is often considered to be of greater benefit to the Divine Plan to continue channelling through that person. The dedication and pure intention of the majority of the people channelling is acknowledged and deeply appreciated by the higher realms. In many cases it takes a lot of preparation, work and much courage to undertake these agreements.

Another point that needs to be considered is that just because a part of a particular channelled material resonates as true, it doesn't necessarily mean that the rest of the content is correct. It is even possible to have 98% truth and still have something in the other 2%, either accidentally or deliberately, that could throw you off on a tangent. You need to be alert to your own guidance. This point would cover all areas of written or spoken communication, whether channelled or not.

As with all communications, you can easily establish if it feels right, if it is loving, uplifting, healing and is assisting you to move out of the third density illusion. In order to fulfil your mission and ascend, you are detaching now from the third dimension. When you emotionally detach, you find you can be far more effective with your help. You will find you will be of far greater assistance when you can operate in a spiritually compassionate and loving way, instead of being caught up in the lower ego's emotional and mental turmoil.

Some material is channelled with the intention of throwing you off the focus of your task. One example of this would be if you were given to believe you were a particular identity (often a well-known Ascended Master) and given lots of 'proof' to back this up. It is very easy from this point to be convinced that you have a special mission and go off on a wild goose chase. You may also be told things like you are "balancing out the whole energy for the planet" just by being here and need to stay still and do nothing. It is very easy to believe these types of communications, as often there is some part of the ego that is delighted. It is usually made to sound so totally correct and logical, that you really need to be in a very discerning space to spot it. It is also easy to believe because you are one of millions of people here with special missions. Without ego, most are just getting on with the job. You do not need to be told through channelling what your mission is, just use your own feelings of rightness and excitement within.

There are currently many lightworkers who have been told they are really Jesus, St. Germain, the bride of Christ, having a spiritual baby to allow someone special to birth, etc. Some are told to tell everyone, thereby losing their credibility and effectiveness as a lightworker. Others are told to keep it to themselves, retreat and do nothing at all to prepare themselves for some future event. There are many variations, but most are made to feel they are 'very special'. The end result of anyone buying into this is that their particular true role here is greatly affected and hence the overall task. Other lightworkers' tasks are also affected, as they have to bear the brunt of the extra workload of the failed agreements and tasks. Everyone has been well trained in the tasks they have agreed to carry out and when someone else has to do it, it is not so easy for them.

Simply perceive the intention of the channelling and always follow your own inner guidance.

If you cannot get the clarity you wish, have a broader look at it. Ask yourself – what will happen if it is true and I follow it? What will happen if it is not true and I follow it? Is there something else that feels more right for me to be doing? Remember it can be very subtle and a pattern can be sneaked in before you know it. Be willing to admit you may not have got it quite right, as only then can you correct it. Are you currently doing something just because someone whom you felt had the authority or that you felt should 'know', told you that was what you were meant to be doing? If it is truly correct, you will feel deep within that it is right for you.

Watch out for the ego. It is always easy to see the difference between the goals of the lower ego and higher Self, if you are honest with yourself. Are you excited because this is truly your path and without any thought or desire for yourself. Does it feel right to work with this to greater help and serve humanity? Does the excitement stem from the ego because it may bring more love, fame and honour into your life? You can ask yourself if you would still want to do this, if absolutely no-one ever knew you were doing it or had done it. Be willing to search deeply and be honest with yourself. If you find it was ego originated, you can put in the discipline necessary to bring back guidance from your higher Self.

In this time of great change, there are many people of different evolutionary viewpoints becoming a part of the new age. Whilst the vast majority are working through love and good intent, there will be a few whose main intention is to make money. Perhaps some will deliver workshops and lectures from a place of ego. Simply allow these people their place of evolution and love them as you would a child who has yet to learn and realise that the percentage of these people is very small. These all present wonderful opportunities for you to practise discernment, unconditional love and to become a master. Everyone in our lives presents a learning for us.

Some workshops these days offer assistance to open up to channelling. Discrimination is really needed in this area. You will usually find that abilities such as accessing energy, becoming multi-dimensional, accessing the Akashic records, becoming clairaudient (hearing) or tuning into the higher levels of truth come in their right time. You will find that if you need a particular ability, it is presented to you by Spirit. It may be that a particular workshop, technique or book is being presented by Spirit and gives you a feeling of excitement and rightness. This may be showing you the way you have chosen to gain this ability. Ensure it is Spirit that is presenting the excitement and not the ego.

In taking part in any workshop or technique that opens you up to being in telepathic, or any other contact with discarnate beings, realise that it is your responsibility to ensure that the being does indeed work for the Light. You may also wish to establish they are of the highest level you are able to contact.

Understand that you have free will and choice in everything, including which beings you **choose to invite into your space.** No guide, angel or master has the right to override your choice, therefore you should not expect that your errors in discernment will be corrected. It would be wise not to assume what you are being told is necessarily correct. The person leading the workshop may have the very best of intentions, but have little understanding of Universal law and have not checked their own source of communication. Even if they have the whole area in perfect light, the responsibility is still yours concerning any procedures you undertake. You are a master. When you fail to act as a master trusting your inner knowing, it is very easy to decide that others must know what they are doing and blindly follow them.

Surrender yourself to highest Divine Order. Precede this, by calling in your 'I Am' presence. Using discernment and the Universal challenge, you can receive wonderful communications from high level beings. If you feel that you may have allowed someone in your space that you no longer want there, you can remove them. First you need to be operating as Spirit and not caught up in thought or emotions. Then order them out – in the name of God – never to return (three times). **You may need to officially break any agreement you may have made with them, either recently or in the past.** There is no need for fear. You are in complete control of your life, no-one can exert any control over your life without your choosing it.

Protection

In general, providing you are focused in and on the Light, you are usually protected. However, if you are not totally free of negative thoughts and patterns yet, there is a possibility of attracting some interference.

Move into your own power and walk without fear. All are children of God and whilst walking on the Path of Light, you draw pure Light around yourself.

In situations where you feel extra protection is required the following methods may be used:

1. Call forth the gold ray of Christ (three times). You can access this directly or you can ask your 'I Am' presence to bring forth this ray for you. Example, "In the name of God, I call forth my mighty 'I Am' presence to access the gold ray of Christ for my total protection." (Repeat this twice more.) Then say "So be it. It is done" to bring it into the now. The colour gold (the 10th ray) is a wonderful protective shield.

2. Everyone is capable of reaching their 'I Am' presence, by quieting the mind and calling, (as in 1 above). Being more connected to your 'I Am' permits easier access to the higher realms. You can always call on the Ascended Masters and Cosmic beings, either individually or as a group, for assistance. When requesting assistance from the higher realms, keep in mind that you are a master who would not feel the need to beg or plead for assistance, feeling it was perhaps more natural to simply ask with authority. If you think about it, someone in a pleading or begging frame of mind is not being very causitive in their life.

3. The sign of the cross, the name of Jesus and God or any long established name that symbolises God or Divine creation, carries great protective power. You can visualise crosses all around you (don't forget underneath).

4. 'Kodoish, Kodoish, Kodoish' is a powerful ancient protection prayer, meaning 'Holy, Holy, Holy'.

5. Flood yourself and your entire auric field with Light. Intuitively gauge how far out this field extends. You can visualise gold and white Light passing through you.

6. You can request assistance from your angel guides. "By Divine decree, in the name of God, I hereby empower my angelic guides to bring me total protection". (Repeat three times.)

7. Use the Right to Challenge and use it in a powerful way with the authority vested in you – as a master.

8. Break any agreements you may have made either recently or in the past, with the entity or situation you are encountering. "Under Universal law, in the name of God and under the Law of Grace, I hereby break any agreements I may have made with you/any entity that is negative and detrimental to myself and my Service to God". (Repeat three times.)

9. Call in the Archangel Michael of the Blue ray (Divine Will of God), to use the flaming sword Excalibur, to sever the connections between you and that which is disturbing your peace and hindering your service to God. Again the requirement of asking three times applies.

10. 'I AM' sealed forever in the peace, protection, security, love, wisdom, power, supply and freedom of the 'Light of God that never fails.'

11. "I AM That I AM." "I am the presence that nothing ever opposes." (Repeat over and over.)

12. Visualise the Archangel Michael surrounding you in the Blue ray of the Divine Will of God. (Repeat the following affirmation, as a master using the power bestowed of God.
"Lord Michael to the left, Lord Michael to the right, Lord Michael above and Lord Michael below. Lord Michael beside me wherever I go."

13. Place yourself inside a circle of cleansed crystals (choose intuitively), interspersed with about four white candles. Wear white clothing and sit on white material.

14. The infinity symbol – the horizontal '8' – has an incredible power. Use it to seal forever any action you undertake. You can visualise it also in gold. Use it intuitively to ensure its correct use. Only ever use it in Divine service and with unconditional love. Most symbols have their own inherent power. You can always use intuitively any symbols you feel an affinity with and avoid

those that do not give you a loving feeling when seeing them. The Egyptian ankh and the swastika are said to be possible deviations of the cross and circle. Remember the equal cross was in use long before the crucified cross. Some of the Egyptian symbols have a dark energy history.

15. To ensure protection generally, the best way is to raise your own vibration to a level that will not permit lower level interference. To achieve this, you need to ensure that you have higher frequency energy in your space. The following will help attain this: wearing white or clear pastel clothing, playing peaceful high vibrational music, burning white candles, using essences and essential oils, quiet times, soaks in bubble baths, eating fresh light foods in small quantities, a well lit home – either with sunlight or electric light, drinking plenty of good quality water, using as many natural products as possible, including shampoo and toothpaste, doing the things that you enjoy, watching light-hearted films, laughter, wearing colours that suit you, loving yourself, smiling, realising that you are a worthwhile and valuable person, walking in nature, waterfalls, using furniture made from light woods, an orderly home, organised paperwork, bright cheery friends, watching stars and sunsets, loving everyone, hugging, animals, treating yourself, vases of flowers and indoor plants, a mowed lawn and tidy garden with flowers. Avoid all heavy dense locations, old heavy furniture, dark coloured house and office furnishings, violent movies, dark clothing, newspapers and TV news, chaos in your space, storing old papers and objects, heavy meals, processed food, chemicals and negative people.

16. If you are ever in real difficulty, no matter how great the distress, use the OM (AUM). The power of the sacred universal sound of God that holds the Universe in balance and harmony, will also bring **you** back to a state of peace and balance. **Let go and let Spirit direct it** into its correct frequency and power, for as long as it is needed. Even if you felt you were going insane, in the middle of a psychotic breakdown or nearly dead from spiritual exhaustion, this sound will pull you out.

You may have heard of a group referred to as the Greys. This is a group of beings called the Zeta Reticuli, who are greyish in appearance. The abductions of humans for the purpose of medical investigation that have been carried out by this race, have been extensively written about and exposed. An agreement was made between the Zeta and a past American government, permitting them to abduct a number of American people in exchange for technical information. The agreement was later broken by the Zeta, who carried out many more abductions than agreed and also extended their abductions to people of other countries. The American people were initially used because they are an amalgamation of many different nationalities which has altered the chromosome structure, making it stronger. Some people were abducted, samples of tissues and fluids taken and they were returned. Others were taken to the Zeta's planet, permanently. The reasons for the abductions was that the Zeta Reticuli, as a race, were becoming weak and the planet was in difficulty. They needed a strong genetic boost. The combination of the human and the Zeta genes, was to produce a stronger race. Looking from the 'future', this succeeded as a programme. The outcome was an intelligent, caring race called the Essasani. Some of the beings from the 'future' race of this planet are currently helping Earth with her birth into full Light. To understand how this is possible, involves the concept of time being an illusion and the 'eternal now'. There is a higher picture to everything.

Although these abductions were very unpleasant, they were always done with the agreement of the individuals concerned (not usually consciously). The abduction usually managed to release a great deal of buried fear. Often this was the reason for originally agreeing to this experience. Everything in the Universe is done by agreement, often made pre-incarnation or on a higher level and is therefore not consciously remembered. There are still some magazines creating a lot of fear and hopelessness regarding the Zeta. Actually, these abductions are finished, except in a couple of areas where this is still being created as a fear and reality by the local inhabitants. Realise that some people like to feel important and create fear. Belief patterns and fear, both need to be released. If anyone feels frightened that they may have made such agreements or thinks they may experience contact with these ones, you can let the fear go. It is sufficient to simply break the agreements as in number 8 of the protection steps.

You are far more advanced, have more abilities, more power and are wiser than you could even begin to acknowledge. During this incarnation alone, especially over the last few years, you have achieved major cleansing of the lower subtle bodies which contain thoughts and emotions. Even if you feel you can't be doing very well because you are going through great emotional upheavals, it may well be you have reached the last and deepest areas to be released. All this clearing means that your vibrational rate is now much finer and lighter. In this more advanced state you won't need techniques that you may have found useful years ago. It is necessary to acknowledge your new state of being. If you do not realise where you are now, there is a tendency to mistake your current higher abilities (such as detachment) for a lower problem that needs to be handled.

Techniques you need will feel right to you, but may now only take a fraction of the time you once needed. **Agreeing to techniques that are no longer appropriate, will lower your vibration rate.** Your chakras, for example, are vibrating now at a much quicker rate, at higher pitched sound. They would **not** then conform to the old pattern of density or tone (every vibration has its own colour and sound). You also have five extra higher chakras in varying stages of activation that are attuning you to the higher dimensions and which need to be kept balanced with the lower chakras. Provided you are listening, your intuition will tell you whenever you are presented with something that is no longer right for you. Don't be afraid to speak out and say that you prefer not to do this because it doesn't feel right for you. It is better not to do it, than hope it will be all right.

When you incarnate, your higher Self remains on a higher dimension with easy access to greater levels of truth. If you had, for example, evolved to the fifth dimension prior to coming to Earth on this mission, you could have an aspect (or part) of yourself in the fifth dimension, another in the fourth and you, of course, in the third. The higher the aspect, the broader the picture and the purer the truth.

All the Ascended Masters, Archangels, White Brotherhood, etc. follow the same pattern. They may have many aspects of themselves in the third dimension. Some people, believing themselves to be a particular master, could really be an aspect of that being. This would mean that at some future point, when they chose it, they could merge and rejoin the higher being of themselves. The same thing applies as people join up with their 'I Am' presence. The best way to explain this merge in practical terms is that it still feels like you, only now you are you, true Self, not just the incarnated part of you. This is an absolutely incredible feeling of total freedom, complete strength and universal love for all. You will feel very big. There is certainly no need for fear concerning this process. Everything in the pure truth of God's world operates with love and is always acceptable to you.

Looking at this area of aspects, it is possible to contact beings who give their name as one of the Ascended Masters, but he/she could be a 4th, 5th or 6th dimensional level aspect. They would be quite within their rights to give this name, as it is the truth. They are not currently known by another identity, as they would be if they were incarnated. If you wish to establish what level aspect you have contacted, you would need to ask. There is a particular method to this, covered shortly.

There is also a false hierarchy and each of the true Ascended Masters of Light also has an impostor using their name in the lower dimensions. These ones give out misinformation, misdirect mission tasks and promote fear. If you ask why this is permitted, free will and choice exist for all. There would be no concern, if everyone practised discernment. There are some who have blindly branded the New Age as bad, through their failure to recognise this false hierarchy who use negative energies. All answers will be found in love and tolerance and listening to the voice of God within.

The Right to Challenge is a part of Universal law. It is the right to ask of another being his or her intent, identity, etc. The question you are asking, needs to be asked in the same words, three times. To comply with Universal law, it must be answered in truth somewhere in the reply. If you want to check that a being you are in telepathic contact with, is indeed from a high dimension, you would ask the question three times and expect three affirmative answers.

Always using wording that is aligned to the Power of God, an example of procedure would be:

"In the Name of God, Creator of the Universe, I ask are you a/the true master of Light, ...?" (e.g. St. Germain)

"Yes", or "Yes, I Am", or "I Am", or "I Am (St. Germain)" (or similar answer).

Repeat your question exactly.

"Yes", or "Yes, I Am" or "I Am", or "I Am (St. Germain)"

Repeat your question exactly

"Yes", or "Yes, I Am", or "I Am", or "I Am (St. Germain)"

Often the clearest answer is a simple 'yes' or 'no' and you can request this form of answer. If the answer is "I AM", make sure there is no quiet 'not' at the end.

You could then establish the dimensional aspect of that being by phrasing a question such as:

"In the name of the highest Divine Light, I now ask this same being, what dimension are you in and what is your intention in communicating with me?" The procedure of three times always applies.

It is not sufficient to ask, "Are you of the Light?" Many mischievous beings in the astral plane are of the Light, but will give you very misleading information, just to play a game.

You are advised not to accept answers such as "This is a test. You should know" or "I can prove I am your guide/ a master, etc. I can tell you all about your life" (just about anyone can get this information by tuning in to the fields around you or the universal records). You only want **three affirmative answers.**

This challenge should be asked each time, even if you regularly communicate with someone, until you truly know their vibration. It may seem a bit of a nuisance, but it is well worth the trouble. It is also expected procedure, welcomed and highly desired by the Hierarchy of Light. This is because they have a great understanding of how the practice of discernment by the Light Force could produce an instant leap in the Light proceedings on Earth.

If you haven't been using this procedure, you could challenge your own guides and any long established connections you have made with discarnate beings, just in case you are being led astray. More than likely, the beings you are reaching are truly wonderful and here to help. If they are truly of the Light, they will appreciate you being responsible in this area. Beings of Light will certainly not feel insulted or get upset about the checking procedure. Don't buy into any attempts to make you feel guilty about doing this. Universal law exists for the greater good of the Universe.

Every being has their own special vibration and this is how we recognise each other on a spiritual level. There will come a time where you will feel you can recognise the being with whom you are in communication with. When you are completely satisfied with this, you could forgo the challenge.

Regardless of the challenge, your priority will always be your ability to perceive truth and to establish whether the information you are being presented resonates as true and to accept only this. The main thing to remember regarding channelling and protection, is that you have a great capacity for intuitively knowing whatever you wish to know.

As you become more multi-dimensional, you will access truth directly from the Source and not through any specific being or energy. It is not essential to your awakening or your evolution, to be able to channel telepathic communications. It is only necessary to be able to receive Light.

You can easily know anything that is necessary to your service role, by simply reconnecting to the Source, where access to all truth is found. When you are operating as Spirit, everything that you need for your highest good will be presented to you in each moment.

You are a Master walking in the pure Light of Divine service and dedication to God, with total control over every aspect of your life. Born of Unconditional Love, you are invincible and can deal with anything in the Universe with but a gentle whisper of your power.

CHAPTER ELEVEN

Twin Flames, Soul Mates – and Going Home

A Twin Flame/ Divine complement is the other half of you. In the past we have called this our soul mate. We need to redefine this term, as both exist. The term twin has nothing to do with the physical birth of twins. At a certain point in evolution, each soul divides into a feminine and a masculine energy and begins learning along two different paths. You may perhaps assume that your twin would be very similar to you, but this is not so. The two learn in quite different directions, so that when final joining takes place, the learning each has done is gained by both. They complement each other. After the separation takes place, they join up only very occasionally, sometimes in physical form. The main purpose in making this reconnection, is to reflect back to one another that they have reached a certain point in their evolution. This learning continues until each has completed all the learning that can be obtained in this separated form. At this point they would feel integrated and complete within themselves and would no longer feel a great **need** to be with their twin or anyone else.

For the more evolved soul it is normal for only one twin to be physically incarnated in the same time period. The other usually remains discarnate in order to help balance the energy of their twin. This allows an easier time for the one who is incarnated. This lifetime on Earth is the last physical incarnation for all the 'old souls'. There are a lot of people currently thinking, "I hope this is my last physical incarnation!!" Except for a very few who chose to do one more incarnation on Earth after its transformation, the majority wish to return to the higher realms. As the people on Earth will be living in peaceful coexistence, the Light Force assistance will not be needed. If you are groaning at the mere thought of a further incarnation, it is unlikely that you have chosen to stay. Answers are always to be found by asking oneself "Does it make my heart sing or sink?" To complete everything in this incarnation means a great energy balancing must take place in each soul. Because of this, it is even more necessary than usual for only one twin to be incarnated. Only 4% have both the twins incarnated and these are often in two different locations on Earth. The percentage increases slightly for the souls who have not yet completed the learning obtained from being separated from their twin. It requires quite an adjustment in energy balancing when twins meet, so it is not often the two are together in physical form.

You may feel sad to think your twin may not be incarnated at this time, because you wish to share your life with them. This can reflect an incompleteness still present within yourself. Actually you are sharing your life with them, though not in physical form. You will find that your considerations of need, loss, time and space are of a third dimensional nature. The idea that you are only with someone if they have a body that can be seen, is not the viewpoint of Spirit. All twins are in energy contact, the degree of this depending whether you are awakened and vibrating at a sufficient frequency. Many are in telepathic communication with each other. There is no Divine law preventing anyone being in total communication with their twin. You can ask your 'I Am' presence or the Ascended Masters to assist you with this.

The love between the twin flames cannot be described in the language of Earth. It is an absolute state of unconditional love, and beyond the capability of any being whilst incarnated, to envisage or experience this incredible level of love in its fullest capacity. After incarnating here for an extensive period it is sometimes hard to conceive of that magnitude of love. There is absolute love present. As well as this, imagine a situation where you know and understand a person so completely that there is nothing they could say or do that would ever upset you. This is because you clearly see the infinite path that has led you both to this point.

Soul mates are several in number, often between 6 and 12, and it is these beloved ones of our core soul family that we often incarnate with in very close relationships throughout many lifetimes. They are often the mothers, spouses, brothers and close friends that assist us greatly in the learning and growth process.

Because a great love exists between soul mates one can easily be mistaken for the twin flame. While not many twins are incarnated, each lightworker has several or more soul mates incarnated and many are destined to be together. In this last physical incarnation many soul mates are helping each other bring up the deeper levels of emotion that need to be released. It often requires someone as close as a soul mate with the great level of love that exists between the two to be able to get deep enough to raise these buried areas up to be viewed. If gentler tactics do not work in releasing these areas, sometimes it is necessary for one of the soul mates to leave the other. This can be quite devastating and usually seems incredible to all concerned, as often the high level of love between the two people is apparent to all. This is often judged harshly both by the mate being left and various friends and family. It is however a great act of love, often only willing to be undertaken by soul mates. If you consider the larger picture, you are then able to see the absolute necessity behind such a move. The larger picture involves the twin flame and the completion of life on Earth and one's ascension.

Old Souls

These missionaries have travelled long and far in their learning separated from the twin. Now for all the 'old souls', the journey is completed and no further separation required. Now the two re-join each other and will continue their learning side by side, through the evolution of the higher dimensions.

Starseeds are only a percentage of the 'old souls' that are incarnated on Earth. All the 'old souls' on Earth are completing their last physical incarnation – ever. If any planetary system needs assistance in the future it will be undertaken by others needing to learn.

Upon completion of the exquisitely beautiful stage of ascension, this time the twin flames are **reunited forever.** They may now do whatever they wish, including returning home. Home can mean different places to different people because the evolution of each being is different. Wherever it is, be it a dimension, planet, galaxy, another universe or a return to the Throne of God, it is that deep place of the heart that gives you an incredible feeling of rightness and warmth within. You may have had moments in your life when the memory of this place was triggered and you felt a deep longing, sadness or a strong desire to be somewhere you couldn't quite consciously grasp or define.

Other Missionaires

Those members of the Light Force who are not 'old souls' will still connect with their twin flame at their ascension. The difference with these ones is that after a while they will see the great benefit to both of them to finish the learning that can only be obtained whilst being separated. So at some point they will probably separate again for a while until this is obtained and then they too will join forever. This applies only to a percentage of the Light Force. The time involved to complete the learning may be very short. In the highest truth of course, there is no such thing as time or separation. This period of separation of the twins would also be the general evolutionary pattern for the rest of humanity, who would still have some learning requirements that needed separation from the twin.

The Light Force of Earth

As each Light missionaire completes the requirements to ascend (Chapter 6), with mission tasks and all agreements now completed, they join their twin flame/ Divine complement and the two make their ascension together. They move through a process that is known as the Ascension Flames which is a Light energy of transformation. The Ascended Master Serapis Bey is the overseer of this ascension ceremony, which uses the fifth ray's white transformational energy of purity.

It may be that you and your twin decide to have an incredibly long holiday (like an eternity or two!) after your mission work here. Realise the deep tiredness or weariness you may be feeling as you come to the end of this long mission, will disappear as you pick up your empowerment and move toward ascension. You are feeling this weariness particularly now, because it is coming to the surface to be released. Even though the weariness will be released, this doesn't mean you will be off on another mission. For some 'old souls', just the thought of another mission produces groans! They probably feel they want a long period of total peace. Remember that truth brings excitement and enthusiasm, so if the idea of going on another mission doesn't excite you, it can't be truth.

As all creation is instantaneous in the fifth dimension and above – you can literally create anything. If you would both like to share a few hundred years (or five minutes) in a wonderful tropical island paradise, with breathtaking sunsets over magnificent oceans, in the exquisite colours that one sees in the higher dimensions, it is but a thought away. If you wish to either go home or rush off to explore the possibilities of new service roles, it will be so.

If you can dream it, you can have it.

CHAPTER TWELVE

Ten Steps to God

You will complete all the tasks you have undertaken concerning your purpose here.
You will carry out all agreements you have made with others.
You will easily see the lessons you need to learn.
You will bring all your energies into balance (including any karma if needed).
You will have all the abilities and powers you need in any given moment.
Your life will be positive, fun, rewarding, fulfilling and full of love.
You will become a multi-dimensional master.
You will bring all the lower subtle bodies into Light.
You will become the God qualities you have chosen to reflect on Earth.
You will complete your mission.
You will attain your ascension and experience the greatest inner joy and excitement imaginable.
You will join with your twin flame.
You will go home (if this is your choice).

If You Can:

1. **Maintain a balance between Heaven and Earth.** This is achieved by being neither too spaced out nor too grounded. If you are 'spaced out' you cannot easily perceive what is being presented to you in the 'now'. You simply aren't there to see it. You will also have difficulty coping with everyday life and will probably be disorganised. This will be obvious to everyone around you. If others see that you can't manage to keep appointments and you are forever losing things, will they choose to follow you? When you are too earthed or

'grounded', it is difficult to reach into the finer, higher frequency energies to gain access to the spiritual realms. The lightworkers are meant to be leading the way, showing their love and Light as a beacon for others to follow. This can be achieved by maintaining a balance in your life. You will also need to be balanced in order to ascend.

2. **Be in the moment.** Do not dwell on the past. If your attention keeps turning to the past, perhaps some experience needs to be let go and released up into the Light. It could also be that your present moment is not rewarding, usually because you are not fully in it. If you find your attention is on future plans, always thinking about what is on tomorrow, next week or month, etc. you cannot also be in the Now. **If you are not operating in the present, you cannot perceive what is being shown to you in each moment, to help you achieve what is required for your growth.**

3. **Stop judging or criticising yourself and other people and situations.** If you find yourself making a judgement or being critical, you are not looking at the higher picture. You can rise above the apparent third dimensional reality and realise that everything you perceive is a lesson **for you.** Things are not done to you; you are not a victim and you cause the things that happen to you. Have compassion and realise that everyone, including you yourself, is doing the best they can with the data they have at that point in their evolution. Realise that you are practising **conditional** love when you judge or criticise.

4. **Know absolutely that you create your own reality and your own world.** There are **no** exceptions to this law. If you totally affirm the reality that you are a master, then **everything** that is not a part of this reality will dissolve. You always create absolutely everything that happens to you and around you. Every person, circumstance, happening and situation in your life is there **for your good** and because you agreed to it and require it, for whatever reason. You do not need to know the reason; that is a requirement of 'mind'. Simply trust that it must be so and be in the moment, willing to perceive what comes to you as 'feeling right to say or do'. It is very easy for us to believe that we create our own reality when our life is running smoothly. It is a greater feat to achieve the same

122   *The Awakener*

viewpoint when things are not going so well. In truth, all
experience is neutral and it is we who decide whether an
experience is 'good' or 'bad'. A lot of testing is done on this
area, to see if we are able to maintain a spiritual viewpoint and
unconditional love, when the 'going gets tough'. Testing is
always done with the agreement of your 'I Am' presence, for
your highest good.

5. **Follow your excitement without hesitation.** Excitement is
the key to follow. This is the feeling you carry within
the blueprint that points the way of your path. It is the
indication of rightness of Spirit. **Does it make your heart sing
or sink?**

6. **Be responsible for every thought and action. Say what you
mean and mean what you say.** Thoughts and words have great
power. As you pick up your mastership and draw closer to
your Divine connection, your words have increasingly greater
power and care needs to be taken. Also with time collapsing,
the time lapse between thinking a thought and it becoming
manifest in the physical realm becomes shorter and shorter.
This is happening on a gradient, to allow everyone to realise
that they do actually create their own reality. The dimension
that this planet is moving toward has no 'time' and therefore
all thought is instantly created. Everyone needs to get used to
this reality. People will soon realise, through personal
experience, that their own thoughts create what occurs in their
life. Be positive and cancel any negative thoughts. Words have
power, and the word 'cancel' actually does this. Another way
to handle negative thoughts and energy is to visualise the
colour violet flooding through the sentence, area, person, etc.
This is using the violet ray of freedom that transmutes negative
energy to positive.

7. **Maintain control of all the lower bodies.** This means continue
to purify the physical, emotional (emotions), mental
(thoughts) and lower spiritual (ego) bodies. These all need to
be lightened up into even higher frequencies, in preparation
for the Light dimensions ahead. **All buried thought and
emotion from this and previous incarnations, will now surface
in order to be released up into Light.** This would be all those
thoughts and emotions that you were unable to view, perhaps

because they were too traumatic and painful. They then remained buried 'in the dark', in a dense vibrational energy. When something is viewed exactly in truth, an exact duplication of the incident is formed again in its own time and space and it disappears. It then becomes available, not as a memory, but as a **knowing** (a 5th dimensional aspect). As these thoughts and emotions rise up to the surface, realise that you have created the circumstances necessary to bring them up **so they can be released.** You can view the content if you wish, but mostly it is not necessary. **Simply let it go.** It would not be wise to bury it again or you will have to create another situation that will bring it back up again. Remember that in this Universe, when a void is created, something will come along to fill it. It is therefore important that if you release a mass of negativity, you need to fill that space with Light.

8. **Allow the ego to blend with spirit.** The ego-incarnated soul identity is now blending with Spirit. The 'I Am' presence is joining you. **Let it be so.**

9. **Love unconditionally.** To love as Spirit means to love everything – all life forms in the entire Universe. This means not just friends and family, but every person, animal, insect, plant, tree, mineral, every drop of water, grain of sand, pebble, blade of grass and life that exists in God's creation. It also means to love yourself. **All things are God in form.** It is truly possible, whilst still on Earth, to love everyone with total unconditional love. There is never a reason good enough to withdraw unconditional love. It doesn't matter what anyone has ever said or done. When you do not love, fear is present in some form at some level. When you love everyone, what else could occur in your life but complete love. This is the Law of Attraction, what you put out follows a curve (like a boomerang) and comes back to you. Sometimes this works instantly or there can be several incarnations in between, but it always happens.

10. **Faith and Trust.** Faith and trust in God/ All-That-Is/ Universal Consciousness and the universal process that provides all our needs, is perhaps our greatest step. Most of us tend to work our way up to total faith and trust in small steps. It will be required in its totality, prior to your ascension.

You may groan and feel that you will never achieve these things, but **you can and you will.** It is you who will decide when. It can start with simple discipline. Begin now achieving what you can of these steps from one moment and then to another. Soon the moments will begin to join together and your life will be moving in the Divine natural flow of all things. For every moment you are in the Divine Flow you will feel an inner excitement or contentment. You will reach a point where this is so evident, you will be immediately aware when you step out of this flow, because the feeling of excitement will disappear.

We are all striving for a perfect balance in every aspect of our lives. We are balancing – the male and female within; the heart and mind; physical, emotional, mental and lower spiritual bodies, right and left hemispheres of the brain; karmic energies; innocence and wisdom; to remain balanced and harmonious regardless of the external circumstances and living in the physical plane, whilst maintaining a oneness and unity with God. You are probably much closer to achieving this complete balance than you realise. Even if a few traumatic situations are presenting themselves and you are feeling strong emotions coming up – recognise that they are probably the last stages of completion for you.

As ego blends with Spirit and personal desires give way to service to others, you will begin to experience a great inner peace. As you move into the harmony of the universal oneness the struggle of life disappears. The love and joy that many search for all their lives suddenly abounds and a great happiness and contentment permeate as you at last feel truly yourself.

Be as God, serving in a loving and balanced way, following the excitement of Spirit in each moment, accepting the cause, power and dedication of Divinity as a master, in total faith and trust of the absolute love and perfection of all Creation.

CHAPTER THIRTEEN

Let Us Be the Light

Let us become the Love and Light, that each may see it as a beacon and follow it with trust and so link with the Divine source.

Let us remember to laugh and have fun. Life is not a burden, it is pure joy. It is entirely up to you.

Let us recognise that we are but channels for the Divine Light and that it is not our ego-incarnated identity that originates the help we give, but the God/ All-That-Is (however we perceive that to be) and that we simply add our humble self to carry it in our own special and unique way.

Let us make the journey from the head to the heart knowing that, whereas the mind may lead us in circles, the heart will lead us home. Let us steer clear of 'shoulds' and 'musts' that stem from the mind and instead stay in the 'now' and experience the intuitive response of the heart with its right feeling, trusting that this is our connection to God and it will lead us to where we are most able to help.

Let us be grateful to each person that we have interacted with in our lives, thanking them within our hearts for being willing to act as a mirror, reflecting to us what we need to learn. Let us know that we magnetise these situations and people toward us to show us clearly those areas of life where we need to be more unconditionally loving, or to reflect positive qualities within ourselves that we may not have recognised yet.

Let us spread only positive thoughts and discipline ourselves in this, realising that as we become more our true Selves, greater care in this is needed.

Let us make no judgement of self or others, for each is seeking to learn and experience in his/her own unique way, to take

125

that wisdom back to the whole. To realise that if there were only one way to do something, there would need be only one person.

Let us channel and spread light across the Earth such as never before. Let us stand fully in our truth, willing and without fear, to speak that which comes intuitively from the heart. Let us be the Self that we truly are.

Let us, who are granted the gift to teach, keep our costs such that many are reached. Let us encourage all to take back their power, to be the master and seek the truth within themselves.

Let us be discerning and align with Light. There are many ways to learn and you may prefer to align your energies with those whose goals are similar to yours. Make no judgements of anyone and maintain unconditional love to all.

Let us trust the higher God aspect of ourselves and have faith that all is well and in Divine Order. To know that we do truly create our own reality and our own experiences, to serve our highest good.

Let us take full responsibility for our actions and thoughts, not just on Earth, but across the Universe, on all dimensions – realising that each action is interlinked with all realms and all beings. But let us also know that responsibility is not a heavy burden, but a joy that comes naturally and with ease, as we become more truly ourselves.

Let us not allow our healing to become mechanical, but allow for fluidity and intuition to guide us through each moment, permitting the flow of Divine energy to move through us.

Let us be willing to release all that is not truly us. Let us permit the releasing of all buried emotions and thought and allow the mental and emotional bodies to integrate and blend into Spirit.

Let us be aware of the other kingdoms with whom we share this Earth; the lovely crystal and mineral world, the wondrous plants, trees and flowers and great oceans, all bringing to us a myriad healing qualities through the exquisite vibration that can reach us all. Let us also remember the world of the elementals that maintains the Earth for us.

Let us seek to assist others to further awareness of a need for love and care of our precious animal and insect world on land and sea. Let us share our world in love with all God's creatures.

Let us, with integrity, speak only that which we know within as true, whilst making it clear to others, that it is only our truth as we perceive it. Each should accept only that which resonates within the heart and sits comfortably in that place of the three fold flame; the love, power and wisdom that resides within us all.

Let us always look higher, to see the greater picture and the Divine Order of all things and not limit ourselves to a third dimensional reality.

Let us also be grateful to the Ascended Realms of Light, angels and guides, mostly unrecognised and unacknowledged, never failing to extend to us the gifts of their energy, presence and love. Let us release our fixed patterns about when, from whom and in what manner we will be presented with Universal Truth. Know that each receives in his own way and that there is no set or right way. Perhaps the angelic world and Ascended Masters of Light reach you in a way that best suits you.

Let us understand the right use of power and truth, gifted to all, as full service to the Light is taken up. Say what you mean and mean what you say.

*Let us realise that to be here is truly a gift of Grace. Know that we may easily reach a place of peace, joy, love and great fulfilment, by realising that it is not my will, but **Thy Will** be done on Earth, as it is in Heaven.*

May Golden Rainbows Light your way Home

Note for the Awakening Team
(A part of the overall Earth mission team)

This section has been written for a particular group of starseeds to assure them that they are not alone and that others share the reality of their experiences.

The following text will probably only be significant to the team who have agreed to these particular undertakings. Even though the other teams are experiencing great spiritual phenomena and going through huge amounts of testing and clearing, they are approaching their multi-dimensionality in a more graceful and loving way than the awakening team (you can almost hear their groans of disbelief, because it may be full of trauma and not feel very graceful!). It is essential that a more graceful clearing approach is used by the majority of the Light Force, for they are bringing into creation a gentle route (like a map) to allow all humanity to make its ascension. It is a delicate operation to manifest this blueprint, which involves creating a pattern using gentle, steady, consecutive steps that form a broad path of Light right across the world. These steps will lead humanity to its new evolutionary goal.

Each mission team has its own functions to carry out, all equally important to the overall mission plan. The awakening team agreed to assist with certain programmes. Although some other teams may have participated in some of the following happenings, most other teams will generally find that they were not involved in most of these functions.

The majority of this team agreed to be awakened and in place across the world in 1990, some earlier. For many that awakening occurred in October 1990. The awakening referred to is a remembering of their mission here, not a spiritual awakening which usually occurred much earlier.

Anyone in that team who was not already fully enlightened, with all their lower bodies cleared, needed to go through a major cleansing and awakening procedure. This applied to many of the team.

Members of the awakening team will have had many different experiences. This will depend on the stage of clearing and initiation they had reached before their awakening, as well as the specific agreements made by them and their 'I Am' presence. The 'I Am' presences joined with them to get these tasks done and to lead them into the initiations that would take them to a point of regaining mastership. Whilst most did experience interference from the astral plane, by far the majority of this period was involved with higher dimensional activity. The state of being you were operating at did not usually involve much 'seeing', but used levels of **knowing** and pure mathematics.

This awakening team generally found themselves 'thrown in at the deep end' in preparation for their tasks, with a series of procedures that all happened in the same period of time of weeks, months or years. Their awakening was often sudden and very dramatic, with the merging of the higher Self, other aspects of self and the 'I Am' presence, with a major cleansing and balancing of all lower bodies taking place. This involved coping with being thrown suddenly into a multi-dimensional world (consciously operating through many dimensions at once). Using pure light energy, without a need for food or sleep, one entered the magical world of knowing and precision higher mathematics. This was intricately entwined with battles across galaxies and even universes; enduring more pain in all four lower bodies than you thought was available in the entire Universe; a traumatic twenty-four hour a day sequence of attacking entities and having everything in the emotional, mental and lower spiritual bodies hauled to the surface and blasted to shreds around the Universe.

As well as this, at the same time a series of initiations and major testings took place requiring great endurance and an incredible dedication and focus of Light. In the process of making a positive connection with the ascended Light realms, one inevitably ran into the false hierarchy of the Dark Lords (usually without realising it), and ended up running the gauntlet of the impostor turquoise ray with its major confusions, misinformation and its attempts to keep you immersed in the colour turquoise. In *The Winds of Truth* channelled by St. Germain in 1966, he says, "Beware the blue-green ray, a sub-ray annexed by the Dark Lords". This isn't meant to imply you can't wear this colour. However, if you feel 'encouraged' to wear a lot of this colour or surround yourself with it, it may pay to check exactly where that feeling or instruction is coming from. If it has been channelled, you will probably have received an extremely plausible reason as to why this is a good idea. Strictly applying the universal challenge should sort out the source.

Although many twin flames are not incarnated now, it is possible that during this time you may have come into contact with your twin flame in physical form for a very short period. This occasionally ended with the death of the twin. Understand that any loss of the twin flame was pre-planned and that the terrible pain and loss that followed, enabled you to clear the emotional body of all the traumatic experience of this and previous incarnations. This traumatic time, wrought with intense grief of great magnitude, brought even further trauma in the realisation that you could not release your cries of pain into the Universe without causing damage. Many quickly learned how to safely discharge this racking pain, through silent utterance and by using mathematics to strategically distribute the energy in safe quantities. Anyone who feels they may have caused harm prior to realising the correct procedures to use, don't worry – the energies were absorbed and transmuted by others into a positive energy form.

For those who experienced this entire scenario, they know it can never be described to others; this powerful, incredible, life shattering, amazing experience, often going on for months or years, when unbelievable events occurred at the speed of light. During that period of multi-dimensional preparation you operated through the Grace of God in a state of knowing, acting in total integrity with God-given powers, absorbing your light body, moving into and becoming the exquisite fineness of the vibration of pure light and experiencing creation from pure thought.

You may have been involved with the following experiences. You may also have been a part of other encounters that are not mentioned here. Many things can't be brought from conceptual form into language, some things may still be confidential and so many thousands of things occurred so fast that they can't all be recalled.

Communicating with and correcting programmes of the main Atlantean crystal under the ocean; using your 'I Am's' specific aura combinations of colour with intricate gold or silver patterning for protection; perceiving all the silver and golden cords; preparing the grid system of Earth using mathematics and the microcosm to represent the macrocosm (mathematically programming a smaller space in order to handle a larger area); using current location such as room and house as borders for mathematical programming; handling the crystals and beings in the denser parts of the inner Earth; both merging and separating with other aspects of yourself; communicating to the rest of the team through a special pre-arranged frequency; either being teleported or apparently teleported to other locations on Earth (absolutely incredible!); being in the dimensions of instant creation requiring every thought to be 100% positive (not a lot of choice!); collapsing perimeters of outer universes in preparation for the new thirteenth dimension; holding the Breath of the Universe; releasing from an etheric level – yours, your twin's or other team member's deeply buried past life traumas; bringing old Atlantean programmes into the present using your ancient huge Atlantean body; the difficult procedures of understanding and locating the relevant programmes needed when required to cover other members' tasks; assisting people to the holiday camp on Orion; moving back and forward in time using precise timing and time tunnels; hitting time and space warps; relocating disruptive entities to the holding Galaxy 634 for release when Earth is in her new dimension; locating Pythagoras for mathematical assistance; establishing your identity by recalling, locating and retrieving a secret object hidden in Atlantis; remembering hidden locations for key information and power wording; using the doorways in and out of the Universe; assisting others during battles to get back into their bodies using the standard Earth programme procedure for entry through the crown chakra; perceiving the mathematical timing required to enter this galaxy; giving the space fleet orders and utilising their computer systems; mathematically setting the pressures of the new combined physical/ light body; handling the bombardment of red synthetic crystals; learning to use a gold shield for protection; 'hearing' the voice across the Universe with the wonderful divine announcement of the Golden Age; being asked to choose between your twin or the

Earth (testing); being required (part of the initiation) to return home to the higher, finer dimensions of light and come back to Earth again (surely making that decision to return showed the greatest commitment and was one of the very hardest of tasks) and then the hours or days of hard work to decrease your size and be grounded into your Earth-sized body again.

Then another unbelievable event took place. After all this testing (without you realising you were being tested – if only you had known!!), after having fought your battles alone – having become hoarse from yelling for help (and swearing) and finally giving up on ever getting any help from the higher realms – suddenly when it is all over, you realise that now you are getting help. This becomes evident after a while, as looking back you realise that there is no way you could have put the pieces of yourself back together alone. Not unless you'd been able to retreat somewhere into absolute peace for some time (like a lifetime or two!)

Peace finally starts to pervade your shattered space and you recognise your own personality again. Some of what occurred begins to make sense. You even start to view the experience as a **positive** one (and that is definitely the most incredible that has happened yet!) Slowly you reach a space where you are starting to think it just may be possible you are going to be able to live as a part of society again.

Now it is time to let go of any fixed ideas you have formed about this whole event. It is very important that you allow the truth to reach you, in order to realise how much it actually helped you. Something very important to realise is that it helped a lot of other people. In fact, it helped the population of Earth and that alone makes it all worthwhile.

Having begun with a thousand-and-one unanswered questions, slowly more pieces fall into place, and somehow you reach a space where you feel the rest of the answers can wait or just don't matter anymore. Excitement starts to mingle with the peace. The recovery is under way. Slowly your credibility among friends and family starts to return, as they see a master has emerged. For those of your family that cannot see such things, just allow them to be. Remember, they got quite a shock also. As you continue operating in the Divine flow of Love and Light, on some level they will recognise and know.

Realise now that along with the great wisdom and truth, you also received misinformation. As much of the data received appeared to be coming from the Ascended Masters, one now needed to reassess all input, going deep within to seek the truth. It was necessary to do a lot of inner work, passing through the distrust and apparency of betrayal, releasing everything not in accordance with Divine order. One needed strength to re-establish faith and trust in the whole process. In reaching to the God Most High, one gained the absolute truth of the loving dedication given for so long to Earth and humanity by the beloved Ascended Masters and Cosmic beings. Thus one passed a major initiation and moved fully into the service role. At the stage of completing one's own understanding of the whole episode, bringing you to a beautiful place of deep truth, you are in a position to really help dispel predictions of fear and chaos. Working in pure truth and integrity, you are now able to spread positivity, certainty and love.

You agreed long ago to everything that occurred. Every part of it was necessary.

You were a bridge, a way-shower, for your fellow teams of lightworkers, just as the rest of the magnificent team on Earth are creating a wonderful bridge of Light for humanity to follow. You were a test pilot and have blazoned a trail, testing the ground and clearing the way for others to awaken and proceed with their own clearing process in a gentler fashion. You need to understand that when you originally agreed to be one of this team, you knew it would be tough, but you also know that you are invincible. Someone had to create a map – a 'known path', as well as clear out any 'opposition'. As you know, it takes quite a while to recover from this 'fast route'. Just imagine if the entire team had to go through that. The recovery time alone, would be detrimental to the progress of the mission.

The other mission teams really needed to approach their awakening more gently, not because they are not tough enough to take a fast awakening, but because the path **they** create is **the one laid down for humanity.** You are adding light to this path as well, but your blueprint is different now and cannot be used really to create this pathway.

You are now carrying the manifested blueprint of the new combined physical/light body for all the Light Force and humanity.

As each lightworker, choosing to transmute their physical form, reaches this stage of absorption, he/she then joins with the existing carriers of this blueprint.

As you have realised, that was just one stage in a series of tasks. By now you will have completed further phases of your mission tasks.

You have joined with your 'I Am'. Regardless of whether you are still at this moment fully combined or not, in future you have a choice of operating with or without this connection. You have replaced ego with the Divine will of God. To the degree that you are able to maintain positive thoughts, you will be combined with your 'I Am'. You may have found that, during this period, the sudden requirement of being combined with the 'I Am' and having to be 100% positive in thought was a great strain. At the end of this period, if you felt you were not at the stage yet of being able to 'never think a negative thought', your 'I Am' would have needed to separate out from you to whatever degree was necessary to maintain absolute purity. Thought produces instant creation in the higher dimensions. The merging of the incarnated soul and the 'I Am' can take quite a period, sometimes years. The time does vary, because each individual differs in his ability to incorporate this energy.

You will probably have by this stage, chosen which abilities to keep in order to complete your mission here.

Now you are awakened, as agreed, and were in place by the end of 1990.

Now you are fully in service, with an absolute caring for every human being and every living thing. The emotional body has been disintegrated during your traumatic adventure and, although for a while it may have seemed as though you will never feel another emotion again, this changes. You will find you have now readopted some emotions to keep you in the realms of remaining real to others who cannot yet identify with detachment. A lot of people identify 'caring' by the display of emotions and do not realise that absolute spiritual love lies beyond the emotional band. You may also be allowing some emotions belonging to your twin or other aspects, to be transmuted through you. The emotions you do take back will be genuine, but in truth your own have been stripped away. This is a high state of being, so do not misinterpret your detachment as a lower state that requires you to work on raising your buried emotions. Any ego or human desires will only now come into play when it is for the highest service to God. They will be presented as required by the 'I Am'.

You made it through. You are not insane (or if you are, there are a whole bunch of us right in there with you!) What is insanity anyway? Often one is deemed to be insane if one sees or hears things that others cannot see and it is not therefore 'reality' as the majority deem it to be. Yes, well, I guess we are top candidates! It takes being multi-dimensional to see and hear things that others can't! The difficulties lie in the initial stage of being thrown in 'head first', before we are able to differentiate between what is actually in the solid third dimension (and consequently is part of the 'reality' of others) and which things you are perceiving that belong to the fourth, fifth and higher dimensions. With a bit of luck, some of the team may have kept quiet until it was sorted out, but this is doubtful. The nature of the events usually warranted contact with friends and family.

Just 'seeing' in the astral plane can be difficult enough. Try telling a member of your family that they can't sit in their chair because someone is already in it! It is the 'white coat brigade' for you. Anyway, eventually you figured it all out and sorted out those parts that belonged to the third dimension. You then got used to the fact that this was all most people could see. You also had to realise that the incarnated souls around you could not see the higher purpose in their actions that was visible to you, and that was tricky! Hopefully, you figured it out and quickly re-established your sanity before they locked you up. Let's face it, it was a trauma for us, but it can't have been too easy for friends or family either. What a shock for them, a normally intelligent, stable person suddenly becoming 'unreal'. They didn't understand it, but how could anyone expect them to? You were having difficulty understanding it! They coped the best they could. Hopefully, they can now see that everything is OK. And so it is. It is all quite amazingly OK now.

You just released yourself from the confines of the physical Universe.

Everything is in perfect Divine Order.

Yes, it was the toughest thing you have ever experienced, but you will only go through it once.

Now you are able to withstand anything in the Universe. Just be your wonderful, loving, dedicated true Self and never compromise that. As you walk now without ego, loving all life, needing nothing and no-one, feeling the wonder and joy and the connection of your twin, know that you are a true child of God.

Inherently within you now, lies an absolute resolve to complete your mission and do everything you can to bring Earth to the Oneness of Love. The moment is close at hand where you will see all life go free. You are but a breath away from being united forever with your twin flame and going Home.

Now you know you are a master. Now you know you are invincible.

'I Am' the Light of God that never fails.

Because 'I Am' Thee and Thou art me,

'I Am' the illumined presence, power and protection,

Drawing into my care every living creature on Earth

Under the protection of the Divine love and radiance of God.

SHANTARN – Sandy Stevenson

THE BEGINNING ....

STARSEED ANNOUNCEMENT

Major Completion – Earth is now functioning on the New Higher Vibrational Leyline System.

On the 25th November, 1996, our beloved Earth gently and quietly slipped free the ties of the denser energy leyline system she has used since the days of Atlantis. Beginning at 11am on 11/11/96 with the new Moon and ending with the full moon energy on the 25th, the Earth Mother worked systematically with the Light Force across Earth to access the codes for the precise mathematical sequence needed to complete the leyline changeover. During the last four days, thousands of lightworkers carrying the last codes, were drawn to the magnificent Cornish coast of England. Here in a special place with the moon's energy shimmering through the ocean waves, at midnight on the 25th, the blue and gold rays poured down through the Atlantean laser crystal and the last of the four corner cords holding the old leyline was cut. Earth stepped free and gently rested upon her new place, attuning joyfully to her new finer vibrational web of golden Light. She now has the springboard that permits the final stages of her ascension, estimated by many ancient philosophies to be completed by 2012.

Begun so very long ago, the Light Force have maintained their dedication in focusing Light into sacred sites and leyline access points around the world. The multi-dimensional purposes of flooding the Earth with Light include – gently cleansing the Earth's physical and subtle forms thus permitting a transmutation of denser energies without the need for major upheavals in its land masses; channelling Light to the evolved inner Earth civilisation who direct it through the crystal and mineral kingdoms deep within the Earth; assisting the release of all emotional bodies; the structure of a new frequency leyline to allow the final stages of Earth's ascension; holding the axis steady and balanced; permitting the re-establishment of the missing energy symbols through the use of crop circles; gently increasing the vibration of the animal, plant and elemental kingdoms and raising the consciousness of humanity.

The new energy grid and leyline system was created 18 inches above the old ones and was then slowly moved down to a position just above the old. This was to ensure that switching from one to the other would not cause disruptions such as earthquakes within the structure. The new system provides the same paths with the same sacred sites, but has a more extensive pattern of finer lines, with a far greater number of access points around the world. This permits Light to be flooded in **from millions of additional new points,** thus greatly speeding up the access of Light.

The new energy grid and leyline structure and the handing over of the sceptres was a vital step in the completion of the Divine Plan for Earth and necessary before any of the original contracted teams could depart. All teams or individual team members will leave when all their own tasks, agreements and ascension requirements are completed.

Words cannot describe the joy and magnitude of this major achievement for the whole Universe.

SHANTARN – Sandy Stevenson

Confirmation Sanat Kumara – Planetary Logos – through the Grace of the Ascended Realms of Light.

UNCONDITIONAL LOVE
Love Without Condition

I love you as you are, as you seek to find your own special way to relate to the world. I honour your choices to learn in the way you feel is right for you.

I know it is important that you are the person you want to be and not someone that I or others think you 'should' be. I realise that I cannot know what is best for you, although perhaps sometimes I think I do. I have not been where you have been, viewing life from the angle you have. I do not know what you have chosen to learn, how you have chosen to learn it, with whom or in what time period. I have not walked life looking through your eyes, so how can I know what you need.

I allow you to be in the world without a thought or word of judgement from me, about the deeds you undertake. I see no error in the things you say and do. In this place where I am, I see that there are many ways to perceive and experience the different facets of our world. I allow without reservation the choices you make in each moment. I make no judgement of this, for if I would deny your right to your evolution, then I would deny that right for myself and all others.

*T*o those who would choose a way I cannot walk, whilst I may not choose to add my power and my energy to this way, I will never deny you the gift of love that God has bestowed within me, for all creation. As I love you, so I shall be loved. As I sow, so shall I reap.

I allow you the universal right of free will to walk your own path, creating steps or to sit awhile if that is what is right for you. I will make no judgement that these steps are large or small, nor light or heavy or that they lead up or down, for this is just my viewpoint.

140

𝕴 *may see you do nothing and judge it to be unworthy and yet it may be that you bring great healing as you stand blessed by the light of God. I cannot always see the higher picture of Divine Order.*

𝕱or *it is the inalienable right of all life to choose their own evolution and with great love I acknowledge your right to determine your future. In humility I bow to the realisation that the way I see as best for me does not have to mean it is also right for you. I know that you are led as 'I Am', following the inner excitement to know your own path.*

𝕴 *know that the many races, religions, customs, nationalities and beliefs within our world, bring us great richness and allow us the benefit and teachings of such diverseness. I know we each learn in our own unique way in order to bring that love and wisdom back to the whole. I know that if there were only one way to do something, there would need only be one person.*

𝕴 *will not only love you if you behave in a way I think you should or believe in those things I believe in. I understand you are truly my brother and my sister, though you may have been born in a different place and believe in another God than I.*

𝕿he *love I feel is for all of God's world. I know that every living thing is a part of God and I feel a love deep within for every person, animal, tree and flower, every bird, river and ocean and for all the creatures in all the world.*

𝕴 *live my life in loving service, being the best me I can, becoming wiser in the perfection of divine truth, becoming happier in the joy of*

UNCONDITIONAL LOVE

Sandy Stevenson

Permission to reprint

THE TWELVEFOLD "SOLAR BEING"

The Twelve Major & Secondary Chakras.

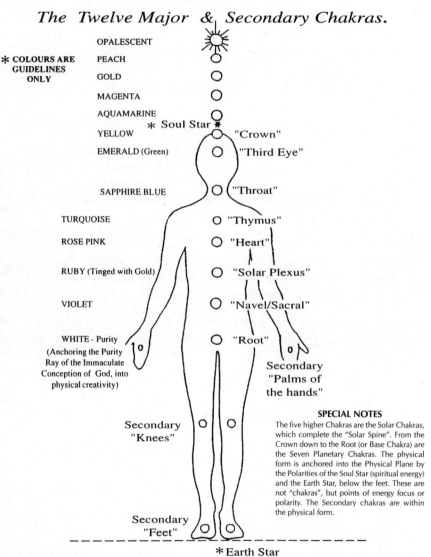

* COLOURS ARE
GUIDELINES
ONLY

OPALESCENT

PEACH

GOLD

MAGENTA

AQUAMARINE

* Soul Star *

YELLOW — "Crown"

EMERALD (Green) — "Third Eye"

SAPPHIRE BLUE — "Throat"

TURQUOISE — "Thymus"

ROSE PINK — "Heart"

RUBY (Tinged with Gold) — "Solar Plexus"

VIOLET — "Navel/Sacral"

WHITE - Purity
(Anchoring the Purity
Ray of the Immaculate
Conception of God, into
physical creativity)

"Root"

Secondary
"Palms of
the hands"

Secondary
"Knees"

Secondary
"Feet"

* Earth Star

SPECIAL NOTES

The five higher Chakras are the Solar Chakras, which complete the "Solar Spine". From the Crown down to the Root (or Base Chakra) are the Seven Planetary Chakras. The physical form is anchored into the Physical Plane by the Polarities of the Soul Star (spiritual energy) and the Earth Star, below the feet. These are not "chakras", but points of energy focus or polarity. The Secondary chakras are within the physical form.

A good exercise is to bring the White Light down through all the 12 Chakras, and into the earth, as a purification.

O'Lean and Elonia. With kind permission.

142

Agreements I wish to break – things I wish to release, so that I may realise my highest spiritual wisdom and power.

I call upon my mighty 'I Am' presence, to fill me with wisdom, discernment and loving intent. So it is.

1. I release any and all expectations I have about my spiritual growth and advancement.

2. I release agreements with my mother, my father, my children, my stepchildren, my husband, my brothers, my friends, my ex-husband and anyone else where this keeps me stuck in a third dimensional reality.

3. I release all invalid concepts about my worthiness of love, joy, peace, harmony, security, abundance, creativity and youthful health and well being.

4. I release the need to save the world or anyone in it. I realise my mission is to accept my masterhood and be a living, loving example to all without any expectations from anyone.

5. I release all preconditioning and all cell-memories about my bodily form. I claim my God-given birthright of beauty, vitality, health and well being, knowing that this is the natural state of being and I only have to follow the nudging of Spirit to manifest this perfection.

6. I release all expectations regarding my creativity. I create from the joy of it and know that my abundance and resources come from Spirit and not from my efforts ...... only from a belief in my worthiness.

7. I release any and all hold that the third dimensional government and establishment have over me. They do not control me, my abundance or security.

8. I release all my residual karmic debts and misqualified energy within me and my physical, mental, emotional and spiritual bodies. I now resolve all conditions with grace and ease and expand into the Light in order to join in the co-creation of heaven on Earth.

9. I release any misconceptions regarding my ability to draw knowledge, wisdom and pertinent information from Spirit. I

   draw on new knowledge and concepts in order to learn and grow and serve by living example.

10.   *I release all judgement, all pre-conceived ideas and expectations for other people, knowing that they are in their own perfect place and evolvement. I give love and encouragement and only offer information when asked and then with the admonition that my truth may not be their truth.*

[Archangel Michael, channelled through Ronna Herman, USA.
With kind permission]

Decree for Ascension

Beloved, Mighty 'I AM THAT I AM', by Cosmic Light command and through all the powers of light responsive to my command;

I invoke my beloved 'I Am' presence, to now take dominion over my life and Light-force, in full power, love and glory, to manifest the completion of my Divine plan, through my Ascension in the Light, with my full cooperation and integration, to express the fullness of my true being.

I AM THE FULLY-EMPOWERED LIGHT FORCE, EXPRESSING THE FULLNESS OF MY TRUE BEING! (3 times)

I AM THE FULLY EMPOWERED LIGHT-FORCE, ACCELERATING MY VIBRATORY STRUCTURE INTO THE GLORY OF MY ASCENSION IN THE LIGHT AND THE FULLNESS OF GOD REALITY! (3 times)

I AM THE GLORY OF GOD MADE MANIFEST, IN, THROUGH AND AROUND MY ENTIRE FORCE FIELD OF BEING AND EXPRESSION! (3 times)

I AM THE COMPLETION, AND I AM THE EMPOWERMENT OF MY DIVINE BEING, NOW FULLY MANIFEST! (3 times)

I AM 'I AM', I AM MY ASCENSION IN THE LIGHT, NOW FULLY MANIFEST! (3 times)

THE LIGHT OF GOD IS ETERNALLY VICTORIOUS AND I AM THAT VICTORY NOW FULLY MANIFEST! (3 times)

I AM ASCENSION LIGHT! (3 times)

I give thanks that it is done.

(Repeat the entire decree three times)

[Channelled from the Ascended Masters by Elonia (Crissie Romano), Australia. With kind permission]

* INVOCATION FOR THE COMPLETION *
OF THE DIVINE PLAN ON EARTH

Through the Beloved 'I Am that I Am', by Cosmic Light Command, and through all the powers of Light responsive to my command, I Decree;

I call forth the God Most High and all Legions of Light Serving Planet Earth, to Complete the implementation of the Divine Plan for the Earth and Humanity – fully manifest now!

I CALL FORTH THE FULL MANIFESTATION OF THE DIVINE PLAN FOR THE EARTH TO PREVAIL OVER ALL HUMAN CREATION – NOW! AND FOREVER SUSTAINED! (3 times)

I CALL FORTH UNLIMITED OPPORTUNITY FOR EVERY LIFE STREAM OF EARTH, TO FULLY AWAKEN AND ACTIVATE THEIR OWN INDIVIDUAL DIVINE PLAN! (3 times)

TO ACTIVATE WITHIN ALL LIFE STREAMS OF EARTH, THE FULL MANIFESTATION OF THE FIRE – FLAME – LIGHT – LOVE AND POWER OF GODS OMNIPRESENCE, OMNIPOTENCE, AND OMNISCIENCE !

HUMANITY IS GOD-EMPOWERED (3 times)

THE EARTH IS CONTINUALLY SUSTAINED IN LIMITLESS COSMIC LIGHT PERFECTION AND PROTECTION – FULLY MANIFEST NOW! (3 times)

GOD IS MY VICTORY! (3 times)

I AM VICTORY – VICTORY – VICTORY!

I AM CONTINUALLY SUSTAINED IN LIMITLESS COSMIC LIGHT PERFECTION AND PROTECTION! (3 times)

I GIVE THANKS THAT IT IS DONE
(Repeat the entire decree three times)

[Channelled from the Ascended Masters by Elonia (Crissie Romano), Australia. With kind permission]

146

THE POWER OF ONE

THE FREEDOM OF EARTH IS WON!
    THE GOD-FORCE IS IN COMMAND OF THE EARTH!

WE ARE RETURNING TO 'THE POWER OF ONE' –
    GOD IS – 'I AM' – WE ARE – ALL ONE!"

WE ARE RESTORING THE 'POWER OF ONE'!
    WE ARE RESTORING THE POWER OF LOVE!
WE ARE RESTORING THE POWER OF UNITY!
    WE ARE RESTORING RIGHT ORDER AND BALANCE!

WE ARE RESTORING OUR QUALITY OF ENVIRONMENT!
    WE ARE HONOURING OUR NATURE KINGDOMS!
WE ARE HONOURING RIGHT RELATIONSHIPS WITH ALL BEINGS!
    WE ARE HONOURING THE GOD-FORCE ESSENCE IN ALL LIFE!
WE ARE RESTORING RIGHT RELATIONSHIP BETWEEN MALE AND
FEMALE!
WE HONOUR THE RIGHT USE OF SEXUAL ENERGY!

WE ARE TAKING FULL RESPONSIBILITY FOR OUR LIVES, AND FOR THE
LIVING PLANET!
    WE ARE TAKING UP OUR PERSONAL EMPOWERMENT, AND OUR
    PERSONAL SPIRITUAL SOVEREIGNTY!

WE ARE – THE COLLECTIVE GOD-FORCE!
    WE ARE – CO-CREATORS!
    'I AM' – DIVINE INDIVIDUALITY!
    'I AM' – THE ESSENCE OF GOD-FORCE!
    'I AM' – CREATIVE GOD-FORCE IN ACTION!
    'I AM' – THE CAUSE, AND 'I AM' – THE EFFECT!

THE GREATEST LOVE OF ALL IS INSIDE ME.

ALL THIS, 'I AM'!"
(repeat three times)

[Channelled by O'LE-AN, Australia. With Kind Permission]

Recommended World Servers

Patricia Dianne Cota-Robles
The New Age Study of Humanity's
Purpose
PO Box 41883
Tucson
Arizona AZ 85717
USA

Cosmic Messenger
Excellent Newsletter 'Take Charge
of Your Life'
Yearly Illumination Congress
Books, cassettes, free lectures
Website:
www.1Spirit.com/eraofpeace
Credit card facilities for ordering

Dennis Stevenson (my brother)
16 Haddon Court
Carrara
Queensland 4211
Australia

*Humorous, inspiring and dynamic
teacher on how to regain political
freedom and take effective
community action*
Former Independent Member of
Parliament
Available worldwide
Beautiful Twin Flame Connection
music cassette
Email: rocket@mullum.com.au
Tel: Australia 0408 625080
(Mobile)

Da Vid
The Light Party
20 Sunnyside Ave, A–156
Mill Valley
California 94941
USA

Cosmic Messenger
Artainment — Video Creation
Numerous Light Projects
Website: www.lightparty.com
Credit card facilities for ordering

Ronna Herman
*Star*Quest*
6005 Clear Creek Drive
Reno
Nevada 89502
USA

Channel for Archangel Michael
'On Wings of Light' and other
books
Excellent channelled newsletters
Website: www.ronnastar.com
Email: ronnastar@earthlink
Credit card facilities for ordering

Robin Bee
PO Box 1454
Byron Bay
NSW 2481
Australia

Cosmic Server
'Starchild' — comprehensive
Ascension
Magazine and cassettes
Personal readings

Edward & Crissie Romano
Gateways of Light
PO Box 153
Perigian Beach
Queensland 4573
Australia

Cosmic Servers
Various books
Temple of Inner Freedom — colour
charts and meditation tape
(A healing journey to an etheric
temple created by the Ascended
Masters to assist all on Earth)
Website:
http://members.xoom.com/gateway
s2012

Avatara Harmony Bottles
Pitt White
Mill Lane
Uplyme
Devon DT7 3TZ
UK

High Vibrational Combination Oils
— channelled from Ascended
realms (this is Vicky Wall's niece)

Tony and Marion Cooper
Aura Light
Rainbow Farm
Buckland Rd.
Bampton
Oxford
UK

High vibrational combination oils
— channelled from Ascended
realms

Shimara   High vibrational oils channelled
Golden Age Reiki Academy   from Ascended Realms
Waveny Lodge   Training
Hoxne
Suffolk IP21 4AS
UK

Sandy Stevenson   For details of workshops and tapes
UK   available
                                         Website:
                                         http://freespace.virgin.net/ascension
                                         2000.web
                                         (no - www - in site address)

Magical Music — Cassettes

John Christian - Seminars and music Relationship workshops
2 Saint Katherine's Cottage   Vocal music cassettes
Green Field Lane   Treks in Nepal
Ickleford
Hertfordshire SG6 1XS
UK

Sally Brown   Musical journey workshops offered
Trafalgar Cottage   to connect to the higher dimensions
Trethillick   Beautiful vocal and instrumental
Padstow   cassettes
Cornwall PL28 8HJ   Altantean language coding -
UK   'Oneness' tape and others
                                         Archangel Michael connection.

Chris James   Beautiful vocal music cassettes
Sounds Wonderful Pty Ltd   Effective, fun workshops learning
PO Box 160   to sing/voice training/teaching
Warrandyte   Email: cjames@chrisjames.net
Victoria 3113   Website: www.chrisjames.net
Australia

The Awakener is now available in German as *Erwachen zum Aufstieg ins Licht,* ISBN 3-502-20230-3.
Available in bookshops or order directly from:
Econ & List Verlag, Munich, Germany